ROOT B

Advertising and Collectibles

DRINK
Hires

The
Honest
Root Beer

Haskell Coffin

Schiffer Publishing Ltd

1469 Morstein Road, West Chester, Pennsylvania 19380

ACLs: Dads, 5¼" h; Connie's, 6" h; CreMel,
5⅞" h; Grandpa Graf's, "1978 limited edition,
600 pc." 5" h.

Published by Schiffer Publishing, Ltd.
1469 Morstein Road
West Chester, Pennsylvania 19380
Please write for a free catalog.
This book may be purchased from the publisher.
Please include $2.00 postage.
Try your bookstore first.

Copyright © 1992 by Tom Morrison.
Library of Congress Catalog Number: 92-60625.

Printed in the United States of America.
ISBN: 0-88740-421-9

We are interested in hearing from authors with book ideas on related
topics.

Title page photo:
Hires tray, tin, 13" h, post-1961. Tray is
inscribed "Hires is a registered trademark of
Crush International Inc."

Contents

Kist sign, paper, 18″ x 27½″.

Acknowledgments

I would like to express my thank you to all those dealers and collectors I have encountered over the years. It has been a pleasure swapping items, stories and friendships, and I look forward to its continuation. My extended appreciation goes to the following for their extra contributions:

A&W Restaurants Inc., Larry Bard, Barq's Root Beer Co., Jim Croan, Dad's Root Beer Co., Tom Eskridge, Ron & Vernie Feldhaus, Dennis Fewless, Foxy's Antiques—Denver, Dave Friedman, Jan Henry, Victoria Herberta, Hires Root Beer Co., Jan Lindenberger, Bill McKienzie, Don McNutt, David & Kathy Nader, Herb Ramsey, Steve Sourapas, Stewart's Restaurants Inc., Marian & John Swartz, Dick Trebilcock, John Vetter, Chris Weide, and Mina Young.

A special thank you to my family for their encouragement and support, and to my wife, Nancy, for her sound advice, understanding love, and tolerance of the collection throughout our home.

Imperial paper label bottle, number of ounces
not indicated. Blob top bottle with "lightning"
wire stopper to lock in cork. Round bottom
required bottle to be stored lying down so
contents would keep the cork moist and keep
it from drying out. The lightning stopper,
combined with the blob top and its seams,
date this one c. 1875-1880. Extremely RARE.

Introduction

Welcome to the world of root beer. Before reading further, take a moment to mentally count how many brands of root beer you are able to name. Over five? Over twelve? Of the hundreds of people questioned, only two could name over twelve brands. None were aware of the existence of over 831 different brands. At least that is the total that I can presently substantiate. No doubt, several hundred more are hidden in a dark corner waiting to be discovered. Of these 831 or more brands, many were "ma & pa" type operations, so tiny and localized that their only product was root beer. Many of the larger, more established companies produced root beer as an additional flavor to their existing line of beverages.

Hundreds of people collect soda pop bottles or mugs and their collections usually include some prized root beers. The same holds true for cans, crowns, dispensers, signs, etc. However, few people collect root beer per se—just for the sake of root beer. This may be due to the public's unawareness of the vast number of root beer brands and the advertising articles used. My ballpark guess as to the number of root beer advertising pieces to be found may well exceed 2000.

A primary goal within my own collection is to represent each root beer by at least one item to show proof that the brand actually existed. Do not assume it is root beer unless the item has "root beer" written on it, with a few exceptions. Older, national companies such as Hires, A&W, and Barqs produced early advertising without stating "root beer" on the product. Simply recognizing their popular logo immediately brought root beer to mind. However, Hires of yesterday sold ginger ale, and root beer companies of today have added other flavors to their line, making it more important than ever that each piece be identified with the words "root beer."

A quick word about root beer schnapps and birch beer. Although I have nothing against them, they will not be included in these works because I consider them to be in a different category from root beer as we know it.

A fellow collector once mentioned that someone should open a root beer museum, and suggested it be called "The Great Hall of Foam!" Well, I have started the wheels in motion and look forward to its reality. I hope she doesn't mind me borrowing and quoting the idea as my own.

May health and happiness always be yours. A root beer toast to you. Meanwhile, have a mug of suds!!

Assorted generic crowns (no brand names).

Hires cardboard sign, litho, di-cut, easel back,
7" x 11½".

Chapter 1
History of Root Beer

Root beer came about in the early 1870s when Charles E. Hires, a Philadelphia druggist, experimented with an "herb tea" recipe given to him by a friend. Claims have been made over the years that Dr. Swett's (originally from Boston) was the first root beer, dating as far back as the 1840s. However, this has never been substantiated (the company may have started then, and the root beer may not have), so Hires maintains the recognition as "The Father of Root Beer."

After serving his new concoction to local friends in his drugstore, Mr. Hires introduced his root beer syrup to the general public at the Philadelphia Centennial Exposition in 1876. Soon thereafter, his syrup was made available to homes and soda fountains. In the 1880s, his root beer was made available in a liquid concentrate; the Hire's Household Extract that became so popular. Of course, other drug companies immediately saw a good thing and began selling their own brand name of root beer extract. Indeed, theirs became only an additional product to an already established drugstore line, while Hires was able to concentrate on a single product which may have been an advantage. History has proven that none of the extract brands enjoyed as wide, or as long a dissemination as did Hires. In fact, most extracts were discontinued by the 1940s. Hires grew to be the largest "home brew" supplier up until the early 1980s when the household extract was discontinued. In 1887, Hires was the first to advertise its product with a full page newspaper advertisement.

Not all of the "secret ingredients" in root beer were disclosed, but those mentioned by various brands included dandelion, ginger, hops, pipsissewa, sassafras, spikenard, black birch, sarsaparilla, elecampane, berries, flowers, etc. During its early years, root beer advertising emphasized the health properties contained therein for the aid of both young and old. The most popular advertising vehicle of the time was the trade card. It not only publicized the 4-6 gallons the "home brewers" could produce for only 25¢, but the cards also highlighted such health claims as: "It acts upon the kidneys and liver"; "Gives an appetite and aids digestion"; "Provides nerve strengthening"; "Has the properties of toning the stomach, regulating the bowels, and purifying the blood"; "Cleanses and purifies the system"; and "Clears up the complexion."

Root beer was called the temperance drink and later, during Prohibition (1920-1933), Hires referred to its root beer as the "Prohibition Beer." Advertising the health qualities was later used for a new product in 1886; Coca-Cola. Early advertising referred to it as "The brain tonic" because it contained some cocaine. The cocaine was removed from Coca-Cola's formula in 1905. (New Encyclopaedia Britannica—Ready Reference. Vol 3, 15th edition. 1989. page 417.)

Soda fountains became very popular after the turn of the century and were found in nearly every drugstore. The attendant for the fountain was known as the "soda jerk," a term probably derived from the person's motions when mixing certain items in a stainless steel container by hand. The fountain was the hub of ice cream, banana splits, milk shakes, sundaes, fountain drinks and of course, one of the more popular items, the root beer float. This combination of root beer and vanilla ice cream served in a glass or mug was commonly called a "brown cow." When chocolate syrup was added, it became a "black cow."

The fountain was a great place to gather and, hence, became an important spot to advertise related products. Fancy dispensers designed to catch the eye aligned the back counter, advertising the syrup contained within: limes, oranges, colas and root beers. Other root beer brands existed at the time that did not provide fountain syrup, and for others, providing the syrup was their only involvement in root beer. The old drugstore, with its marble counter top and swivel stools, began to fade away in the late 1950s. The increase of suburban shopping centers and larger department stores, each containing their own drug line sections, replaced the corner drugstore. A few remain, but not as they once were.

Root beer was first bottled for Hires in 1893 by the Crystal Bottling Co. As bottling plants began to appear across the nation, different brands of bottled root beer began to appear as well. However, the Prohibition era and the 1934 invention of the applied colored-label (ACL) technique on glass really spawned thousands of "soda pop" companies and local bottling plants, and at least 100 different bottled root beer brands. The majority of these beverage companies had a short life span and only distributed locally or regionally through one or two bottling plants. Most brands began as, and remained, small family operations limited to one or a few flavors, which sometimes included root beer. The larger companies, which produced a greater number of flavors, may or may not have included root beer. Surprisingly, even national companies tried their hand at the popular flavor. Anheuser-Busch, Holiday Inn, and Kool Aid are three such companies.

Many of the little known, localized soda brands which may or may not have made root beer, thrived for a brief period. A few local and regional brands still exist, produced by independent franchises, but many were discontinued as small plants began closing. So ended an era and started a collectable! The time of hunting for discarded pop bottles along the roadside and in vacant lots for the 2¢ deposit is long gone. By the time the deposit reached 5¢, then 10¢, the "ma & pa" grocery stores were overshadowed by big supermarket chains and the little ol' pop bottle was no longer economical to produce.

The can was invented in 1934, and by the 1970s, more soda seemed to be found in cans on the store shelves and in pop machines than in bottles. It was common in the 1970s for food chain stores and food processing companies, large or small, local or national, to sell root beer under their own name, such as: Giant Foods, Red Owl, Family Dollar, Food Club, Welch's, Pantry Pride and Target. This practice is not as prevalent today however, as new root beers presently being tested on the market can be discovered in many food outlets.

Root beer is 115 years old. The history of many brands are unknown or sketchy at best. Every so often, one appears from the past unheard of before. They may have been so small that only the local, elderly citizens remember something about it. Minor brands produced very little in the way of advertising pieces, and those that survived the early times of major brands are now becoming scarce. It may be that some root beers never surface to establish their existence, as holds true with any vein of history, from firearms to dolls. Progress is designed to meet the needs of the population, and new methods and improvements are certainly inevitable, but sadly, a little bit of Americana is lost in the process. Each generation retains certain memories of the past, of days gone by, each unique unto themselves. Happily, sometimes through collectors, a lost piece of history is discovered and preserved for future generations to see and enjoy.

What is the future of root beer? Here's what the Hires people said recently: "Root beer has outpaced the growth rate of total carbonated soft drinks during the last two years. It makes up the fourth largest catagory following colas, lemon lime, and orange. The future is certain—Root Beer is here to stay."

Little Known Trivia Facts

"Dennis the Menace," originating as a comic strip by Hank Ketcham, was occasionally drawn serving his favorite meal to his mother when she was sick in bed....a peanut butter sandwich, jelly beans and a root beer. In the 1966 issue of *Look* magazine, a full page ad displayed Dennis demanding A&W root beer for a picnic.

Alvin, one of the three singing chipmunks of the 1950s, is shown on one of their album covers dressed as a cowboy in a saloon drinking a can of root beer.

Louis Ballast, known as the originator of the cheeseburger, was granted a patent for the name "cheeseburger" in 1935. From a small operation located on 29th & Spear Blvd. in Denver, Colorado, his business was considered the first drive-in type in the state and was also the first to employ carhops in Colorado. Information gathered from long-time residents of the area place its closing around the late 1940s-early 1950s. While the drive-in was open however, it was the most popular hangout for the high school nearby. Root beer related? You bet your mug! Known as the "Humpty Dumpty" drive-in, it was built in the form of a large orange root beer barrel. Americana personified!!

The "Gold Cross" embossed soda bottle has an interesting story involving its name. San Antonio, Texas is peppered with missions and churches. Across from the bottling plant was a church with a gold cross on it, in constant view of the employees as they arrived or departed the bottling plant. Inspired by the sight, the brand name came into existence. This was told by a friend of the plant owner. It may or may not be true, but it makes for a good story.

The cartoon dog "Snoopy" from the *Peanuts* comic strip by Charles Schulz had a long-running love for root beer. It was not unusual to see Snoopy on Veteran's Day on his way to "quaff a few root beers"! As of April 1990, Snoopy became the new spokes celebrity for A&W Root Beer with an official title as "The World's Greatest Float Maker."

A hit song by the Country & Western singer, Tom T. Hall, entitled "Sneaky Snake" mentions that Sneaky Snake likes root beer and will get yours if he can!

A&W ashtrays, glass, ACLs. (The left one bears the earliest logo. Notice the two on the left are from the same address, but the owners have changed. The building has been vacated for nearly a decade.)

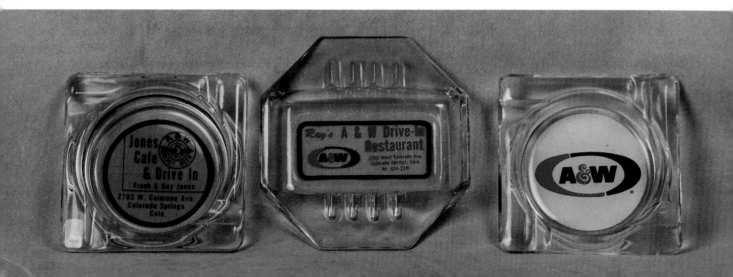

Chapter 2
Bottles

Extract

Soon after Charles E. Hires introduced root beer to the public in 1876, a packaged Hires household extract was made available to homes and soda fountains. Indeed, other companies quickly followed with their own version of root beer extract. None, however, was as popular or achieved the wide distribution of Hires' extract. Hires was strictly root beer, devoting all energies to their only product. To the others, mostly drug companies, root beer was just an additional item to their existing line of products.

In addition to the medicinal properties advertised therein, these bottles held the "secret formula" syrup for making good ol' root beer at home. One had only to add the extract to certain home ingredients: water, sugar and yeast. The home brew was bottled in anything that was corkable,

allowed to set (ferment) several days, and was ready when the corks began to pop.

Trade cards, produced by various companies, advertised that their root beer product produced 5-6 gallons, all for only 25 cents!

The extract bottle, mainly sealed by cork, was found in amber, aqua, or clear glass. Most held 3-4 ounces and ranged from 4-5 inches tall. The majority were basically the same shape and embossed on the sides with the company's name and advertisement. Extract bottles, for the most part, were discontinued by the 1940s. Hires finally ceased United States production in the early 1980s.

Brands represented: (Variations in wording and bottle design exist for some)

Allen's	French's	Nyman's	Three Star
Ayd's	Galvin's	Papoose	Towle's Log Cabin
Baker's Indian	Hallock's	Polar Bear	Triangle Club
Bean's	Hartshorn	Puritan	United States
Bryant's	Heinle's	Raser's	Ward's
Burrough	Herter's	Royal Worchester	Warwick's
Burton's	Hires	Schilling's	Watkin's
Champion	Horseshoe	Shank's	Week's
Dove	Indian	Shrader & Johnson	William's
Durkee	Knapp's	Strickler's	Zatarain's
Favorite	Larkin	Supreme	
Fisher's	Lear's	Taylor's	
Flagstaff	Mexican	Thomson & Taylor's	

Extracts, left to right: Pa-poose; Puritan; Hires; Hires; Schilling (can be found on today's grocery shelves).

Extracts, left to right: Bryant's; Baker's Indian; Indian; Thomson & Taylor's.

Extracts, left to right: Galvin's; Galvin's Yuca; Nyman's.

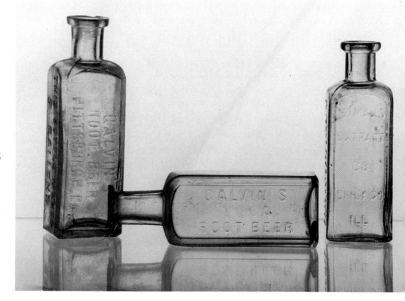

Various Hires extract bottles. The two on the left would be sealed by a cork. The newer bottle on the right is sealed by a screw-on cap.

Knapp's extract bottle. Resembles a tiny pocket flask. Embossed picture of colonial with hat in one hand and a glass in the other. 4⅛" x 1¾" x 1".

Stoneware (pottery)

Stoneware bottles, for root beer purposes as depicted here, enjoyed a peak period from approximately 1890 to 1920, although there have been unconfirmed reports of usage well into the 1940s.

These bottles, occasionally referred to as pottery or clay bottles, had a glass-like finish or protective glaze, and were normally tan, white, gray or brown. Similar to the European "Ginger Beer" bottle, the standard type had a gray bottom half and a chocolate brown top half.

The stoneware bottles used for root beer varied in size and shape, but for the most part they were either 8 oz or quart size. Closures consisted of either a cork or a cork with a lightning stopper (an attached wire connected to the bottle neck which swiveled up and over the cork to secure it in place). Printing was applied prior to the glazing, and any embossing was impressed into the clay before baking.

Information remains sketchy on these beautiful bottles and many questions remain unanswered regarding origin, bottling and limited distribution.

Brands represented: (Variations may exist for some brands)

Boyd & Beard	Krass, Wm.
C. Leary & Co.	Ledger's
De Freesti	Old Colonial
Dr. Swett's	P.J. Cray's
Fargo	Vreeland's Indian
Hires	Wagner Bros.
Hogan, M.	W. H. Gray

Left: Dr. Swett's stoneware bottle, 8 oz. 7½". Reverse is blank. Right: 7¾", reverse is displayed, same front as bottle on left.

Old Colonial stoneware bottle, 7½", cork sealed.

Assorted stoneware bottles, left to right: P.J. Cray's, 8 oz, 7¾"; Hires, 8 oz, 7½"; C. Leary & Co., 8 oz, 7¾". All would be sealed by a cork.

Embossed

During the 19th century, it was common practice by the bottling companies to emboss bottles as a form of identification and advertising. Embossing is the process of cutting desired letters or designs into the inside surface of a bottle plate mold. When the liquid glass is poured into the mold, the result is a raised letter or design effect on the side of the bottle itself. This not only provided for permanent advertising, but also established a means of insuring the bottle's return for reuse. This procedure was also used on early glass mugs.

Although this technique was used well into the twentieth century on early soda bottles and the like, root beer appeared on the scene at a time when the popularity of embossing had declined. It was soon replaced by the applied colored label (ACL) method invented in 1934. Few bottles were embossed with root beer advertising prior to 1910.

Brands represented:

A & W	I.O.C.	Rosebud
Barq's	Jackson	Royal Crown
Dad's	Mason's	Worley's
Farnham's	Pop-Over	Wright
Gold Cross	Portage	
Hires	Purdy	

Reverse of Jackson's. A 2″ diameter embossed picture of General Jackson on his horse.

Jackson's, beautifully embossed, 12 oz. "Jackson Brewing Co., New Orleans" embossed on the bottom. RARE!

Barq's various designs. Left to right: 12 oz, "no refill," c. 1988; 10 oz, c. 1961; 12 oz, c. 1951; 12 oz, c. 1961.

Embossed soda pop bottles: Gold Cross, 10 oz, "Rodriguez root beer and bottling company, San Antonio, Texas" around bottom edge; Rose Bud, 12 oz, roses and vines decorate glass.

Assorted embossed pop bottles. Left to right: I.B.C., 12 oz, c. 1986, "no deposit no return;" Dad's, 12 oz, "no deposit no return", barrel designed; Dad's, 12 oz, "no refill", barrel designed, c. 1987; Mason's, 12 oz "non-refillable," reverse lists states paying a 5 cents refund to promote recycling, c. 1987.

Hires early pop bottles. Left: 9¾″, embossed.
Right: 8¼″, embossed.

Assorted embossed sodas: Left: Wright, 12
oz, "Drink the Wright root beer." Middle:
A&W, 16 oz, "no refill" c. 1978. Right:
Worley's, 10 oz, very dark amber glass, c.
1947.

Paper labels

Although improved methods were invented for labeling bottles, particularly with the applied color label (ACL) in 1934, the root beer paper label never became extinct since it was cheaper to produce than other means.

Prohibition (1920-1933) may have been one of the busiest periods for root beer paper labels. An existing stock of beer bottles was certainly on hand when prohibition began, and since the bottles were amber, they were ideal in preserving the root beer against the sunlight. Also, the beer bottle provided for some, the feeling of enjoying a beer. For others it may have been used to disguise the actual contents under the root beer label!

Lack of information makes it difficult to determine when a certain paper label existed. What may be helpful as a focal point are those labels which indicate 12 oz contents. Pepsi-Cola introduced the first 12 ounce bottle in 1934, and from thereon, the size normally increased (16, 32, 64 ounces, liters, etc). When companies changed to ACLs, the label designs did not change drastically. Liters and bar codes also represent a newer era.

Smaller beverage companies with limited distribution probably considered it more economical to continue using paper labels long after ACLs became available. Wash, sterilize, slap a new label on the returned bottle, and back out to the public it went. The process seemed simple enough.

Brands represented:

Anheuser-Busch	Dad's	Grandma's	Lack's
Belfast	Donner	Grandpa Graf's	Lake Breeze
Black Bear	Dr. Swett's	Greendale	Lee
Blackhawk	Duffy's	Gruenwald, C.E.	Lost Trail
Bobby's	Echo	Hanover	Love
Boulevard	Eclipse	Heinle's Jockey Club	Lucky Star
Brillion	Electura	Hires	Mad River
Bruce's	Elson's	Howel's	Manitou
Campbellsport	5th Avenue Seltzer	Hy's	Ma's
Clear 'OC	Frostie	I.B.C.	Mother's
Cleve 'O Club	Garden City	Imperial	Mug
Clicquot Club	General	Ironwood	Napa Rock
Club Deluxe	Giering's, J.F.	Jo Sole	New York Seltzer

No Cal	San Francisco Seltzer	Standard	Valley
Old Fashioned	Sarsaparilla	Stewart's	Vess
Old San Francisco Seltzer	Schwartz	Swallow's	Weber's
Old Time	Seymour	Sweet 'n Low	Werbelow's
O-So	Singer's	Teddy	Western Bottling Works
Peerless	Soda Barrel	Ting	Win's
Pioneer	Soho	Topp	Winterbrook Seltzer
Red Robe	Sparco	Uncle Dan's	Yankee Doodle
Red Rock	Sparkletts	Uncle Smilie's	Yukon Club

Assorted paper label bottles. Left: Yankee Doodle, 12 oz. Middle: I.B.C., 12 oz, c. 1976. Right: Howel's, 12 oz.

Anheuser-Busch paper label, 12 oz. Busch introduced root beer during the prohibition in 1923. According to the Anheuser Busch archives, this bottle is pre-1939. RARE!

Red Robe paper label bottle. 12 oz, "made with pure cane sugar." Picture appears to be that of a young Roman with a pencil and tablet in hand. Bottle is of black glass and may have been randomly selected for the label since "Mission Dry Sparkling" is embossed on its bottom.

Paper label bottles. Schwartz, 12 oz. and Vess, 12 oz.

Duffy's paper label bottles. Left: 12 oz, "Duffy's" embossed on shoulder, c. 1936. Middle: 32 oz, "Duffy's" embossed on shoulder, c. 1947. Right: 12 oz, amber bottle c. 1941.

Hires paper label bottles, 12 and 32 oz.

Paper label bottles. Dad's 12 oz and Hires 12 oz.

Paper label bottles. Ma's, 32 oz, "Old fashioned" embossed on neck, "The kind that mother used to make" embossed around bottom. Greendale, 1 pt. 14 oz.

Paper label bottle. Manitou, 12 oz. Very RARE.

Paper label bottles. Left: Boulevard, 1 pt. 6 fl oz. Middle: Grandma's, 32 oz, c. 1953. Right: Sparkletts, 1 pt. 13 oz, c. 1950. All three are from the Los Angeles, CA area.

Yukon Club paper label bottle, 64 oz.

Soho paper label bottles. Left: 12 oz, 1986. Right: 23 oz, 1990.

Paper label bottles. Left: Uncle Dan's, 12 oz, c. 1947. Right: Standard, c. 1947 (a label indicating 7 oz seems to be on a 12 oz beer bottle!)

Paper label bottles. Left: Clicquot Club, 12 oz, sugar free. Middle: O-So, 12 oz, "no deposit-no refill" embossed on neck, c. 1973. Right: Topp, 12 oz, c. 1971.

Paper label bottles. Left: Mad River, 12 oz, 1988. Middle: Old-Fashioned, 12 oz, c. 1987. Right: Sarsaparilla, 12 oz, c. 1987.

Various paper label bottles. All 10 oz. Seltzers. Left to right: Old San Francisco, c. 1986; San Francisco, c. 1989; Original New York, c. 1986; Winterbrook, c. 1986; 5th Avenue, c. 1986.

Blackhawk paper label, 8 oz.

Heinle's Jockey Club paper label, no ounce indicated.

Paper labels. From top: Echo, 24 oz.; Red Rock, 32 oz.; Sparco, 24 oz.

Paper labels. From top: General, 24 oz.; Club De Luxe, 24 oz.; Swallow's, 12 oz.

Paper labels. From top: Old Time, 16 oz.;
Campbellsport Bottling Works, 24 oz.;
Western Bottling Works, 6 oz.

Garden City paper label, with matching
bottleneck label, one quart.

Paper labels. From top: Frostie, 32 oz.; Hires,
24 oz.; Win's, 32 oz.

Love's "Oakie" root beer label, plastic,
circular, slides around a 2 liter plastic bottle.

Paper labels. From top: Ting, 2 liters. Pioneer Soda Bottling Works, two types, no ounce indicated.

Lake Breeze paper labels, 24 oz, regular and low calorie.

Napa Rock paper label, 29 oz.; Dr. Swett's paper label, 8 oz.

Weber's plastic label, circular, slides around a 2 liter plastic bottle.

Jo Sole paper label, 16 oz.

Paper labels. From top: Grandpa Graf's, 2 liter; Seymour, 32 oz.; Donner, 6½ oz.

Paper labels. From top: Black Bear, 24 oz.; No-Cal, 2 liters; Werbelow's, 32 oz.

Applied colored labels (ACL)

Soda Pop Bottles (ACL)

In 1934, the bottling industry was revolutionized when the technique of the "applied-colored label" (ACL) was used on soda bottles to identify and advertise. Commonly referred to as "painted labels," this process of baking colored enamel onto the glass was less expensive than embossing and became more popular than paper labels. The method was extended to include drinking glasses, mugs, and ashtrays, among other things.

Many brands had limited distribution within a local or regional area. Those that turn up in old general stores, closed bottling plants, attics, basements, or from dumps are often quite collectable. The most popular bottles display pictorial labels with at least two different colors. The most desirable are the amber glass bottles with a picture. It was believed that dark glass "preserved" the contents much better from the exposure to light than did clear glass. Thus, amber glass was sometimes used.

In 1934, the first 12 ounce bottle was introduced by Pepsi-Cola. In 1948, non-returnable bottles were made available by the bottle manufacturers.

Various generations of bottles may exist. When a brand's label design changes greatly, it becomes a new generation. When slight variations are found, it is not considered a new generation. With some brands, a number of generations, each having many variations, exist. Others have only one generation with no variations.

Brands represented:

A&W	Blanchard's	Cola	Frostie
Adams	Brownie	Craig's	Golden
B-K	Bulls Eye	Crystal	Goody
Baker's	Bums	Dad's	Gran'pa Graf's
Barq's	Carnation	Dr. Stearn's	Green Spot
Barrelhead	Clarion	Dr. Swett's	Harl's
Belfast	Clipper	Epping's	Hi-Hat

Hi-Top	Marvel's	Rex	Tower
Hires	Mason's	Richardson	Triple AAA
Honeymaid	Minnekahta	Rob's	Triple XXX
Howel's	Missouri Club	Rose Bud	Twang
Hyde Park	Mr. Root Beer	Schueler	Uncle Ben's
I.B.C.	Mrs. Lombardi's	Sky High	Uncle Joe's
Judd's	Mrs. Warner's	Smitty's	Uncle Tom's
Kay C	Mug	Sonny O'Gold	Victory
Keen	My Pop's	Sparkeeta	Walker's
Kelly's	Ol' Smoothie	Sparkling	Worley's
Kist	Old Time	Stewart's	Wright
Lake	On Tap	Stratford	YD
Leary's	Papoose	Swallow's	Yankee Doodle
Lyons	Peter's	Ted's	Zetz
M.B.C.	Quaker	Ten-Erbs	
Made Right	Ramblin'	Tom Sawyer	

ACL bottles. Baker's, 7 oz, c. 1940.
Barrelhead, 10 oz, c. 1977.

A&W applied-color labels (ACLs), 10 oz, c.
1981 and 32 oz, c. 1973.

Barq's ACL bottles, 12 oz, c. 1942 and 32 oz,
c. 1978.

Clarion ACL bottle, 7 oz, 1952.

ACL bottles, from left: Bum's, "Good down to the last Root!" 8 oz, 1941; Bulls Eye, 10 oz, 1953; Carnation, picture of a carnation on reverse, 10 oz, 1964.

ACL bottles, from left: Belfast Mug, 6½ oz, 1950; Blanchard's, 8 oz, 1967; Brownie, 9 oz, 1971.

ACL bottles, from left: Clipper, 10 oz, 1954; Cola, 9 oz, 1948.

Crystal ACL bottle, 29 oz, date unknown.

Dad's ACL bottles, from left: "Junior" size (boy winking), 10 oz, 1948; "Mama" size, quart, 1948; "Papa" size, half gallon, 1948.

Dad's ACL bottles. Left: 7 oz, 1948. Right: "Junior" size, 7 oz, 1952.

Dad's ACL bottles, from left: "Big Jr." 7 oz, 1957; "Original draft," 10 oz, 1973; "Original draft," 32 oz, 1974; Double "root beer," 32 oz, 1978.

Various ACL bottles, from left: Dr. Stearn's, 10 oz, 1958; Dr. Swett's, 10 oz, c. 1945; Dr. Swett's, 10 oz, c. 1947.

Frostie ACL bottles. Left: 12 oz, 1988. Right: 28 oz, c. 1969.

Frostie ACL bottles. Left: Elf, 12 oz, 1966. Many small variations of the elf on different size bottles exist, since 1958. Right: "cameo" lady, 12 oz, 1953.

ACL bottles, from left: Harl's, "root beer with that keg style flavor," 10 oz, 1960; Gran'pa Graf's, 7 oz, 1952; Goody, 10 oz, c. 1950.

Hires ACL bottles. Left: 8 oz, 1945. Right: 12 oz, 1960.

Howel's ACL bottles, from left: 10 oz, 1950; 12 oz, c. 1942; 24 oz, date unknown.

Hires ACL bottles, from left: 12 oz, 1961; 32 oz, 1959; "Genuine," 12 oz, 1968.

I.B.C. ACL bottles, 16 oz, 1978, amber glass and green glass. The green glass is more difficult to find.

ACL bottles, from left: Keen, 10 oz, 1944;
Kay C, 12 oz, 1948.

ACL bottles, from left: Kist, 12 oz, c. 1940s;
Lake's, 12 oz, 1937.

Kelly's ACL bottle, 10 oz, 1953.

Lyon's ACL bottles, from left: Lyons-Magnus,
10 oz, c. 1950; "Old Magnus" as cheerleader
with megaphone, 12 oz, 1951; Lyons, 10 oz,
bottle embossed with name in various places,
"Be happy, inside" on reverse, 1956.

Mason's ACL bottles. 10 oz, 1955; 10 oz, 1978.

ACL bottles. Leary's, 12 oz, 1964 (the logo/design in a 1953 bottle is minutely different). Moody's "Made right", 12 oz, 1941.

Mason's ACL bottles. Left: 10 oz, 1950, clear barrel and background. Center: 32 oz, 1953, clear barrel and background. Right: 10 oz, 1950, solid barrel and background.

Mason's ACL bottle, 32 oz, 1955.

ACL bottles. M.B.C., 12 oz, 1966. Marvel's, 12 oz, "You'll love its Creamy Flavor," 1958.

Mrs. Warner's ACL bottle, 12 oz, c. 1952.

Minnekahta ACL bottle, 10 oz, 1952, "Zill's Best."

Mug ACL bottles "by Belfast." Left: 6½ oz, c. 1967. Right: 12 oz, 1959. (a 28 oz bottle exists, same design and logo).

Mug ACL bottles, bottled under auth of New
Century Beverage Co. From left: 11 oz, 1980;
16 oz, 1980; 11 oz, 1979.

ACL bottles. Ramblin', 10 oz, 1980. Ol'
Smoothie, 8 oz, 1959.

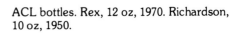

ACL bottles. Rex, 12 oz, 1970. Richardson,
10 oz, 1950.

My Pop's ACL bottle, 12 oz, 1966.

Rose Bud ACL bottle, 12 oz, 1938. "Rose Bud Root Beer" embossed on reverse. Bottle is heavily embossed with roses and vines.

Schueler ACL bottle, ½ gallon, c. 1950s.

Sky High ACL bottle, "Like Mother made," 64 oz, c. 1951. Bottle is designed and shaped like a barrel.

Sparkeeta ACL bottle, 7 oz and 12 oz, date unknown. Picture is of three horses and riders jumping a fence.

Stewart's ACL bottle, 12 oz. This 6-pack was sold on a trial basis in certain cities across the country beginning in 1990.

Tom Sawyer ACL bottle, 8 oz, 1952 and 12 oz, 1963. A quart size has been reported to exist.

Tower ACL bottle, 7 oz, 1951. Name embossed on bottle.

Various ACL bottles, from left: Swallow's "old style," 10 oz, 1953; Swallow's "KEG," 12 oz, date unknown; Ted's, 12 oz, 1958. (Beware of fake reproductions of Ted's. Some were made in 1988 and pictured Ted Williams batting).

Triple AAA ACL bottles, both 6½ oz, 1946.

Twang ACL bottles, 10 oz, 1948 and 12 oz, 1956.

Triple XXX ACL bottles, 8 oz, 1951 and 12 oz, 1944.

ACL bottles from left: Uncle Ben's, 10 oz, c. 1950s; Victory, 10 oz, 1944.

Walker's ACL bottles, 7 oz, 1959 and 32 oz, 1948.

Yankee Doodle ACL bottles, from left: 10 oz, two-color, logo embossed on neck, date unknown; 29 oz, three-color, 1948; 10 oz, three-color, logo embossed on neck, 1948.

ACL bottles, from left: Worley's, 10 oz, c. 1962; Wright, 12 oz, c. 1950s; Wright, 12 oz, 1968.

Chapter 3
Caps and Openers

Bottle Caps (Crowns)

The bottle cap (officially known as "crown") was invented in 1892 by William Painter of Baltimore, Maryland. Because the bottles were handmade, the bottle openings had no uniformity and the crowns did not always fit snuggly. In 1903, a fully automatic machine that made uniform-sized bottles was invented by Michael J. Owens. Painter's crowns then became widely used.

In 1916, thin aluminum discs were used to cover the inside cork of the crown to prevent an off-flavor to the contents. These are referred to as "spot crowns."

In 1955, the first plastic-lined crown was introduced by the Bond Crown Co. Because of cheaper production, the plastic-lined crown soon replaced the cork-lined.

In 1966, the twist-off crown was introduced by the Armstrong Cork Co. With the increase of throw-away bottles, the screw-on cap (aluminum or plastic) became another threat to Painter's crown.

Many root beer brands were strictly family oriented and localized so that the only proof to the company's existence may well have been the crown. The crown is also often the only proof that larger companies produced root beer at one time. Most companies noted the flavor of a beverage on the crown and stated only the company name and the word "beverages" on the bottle. Hence, the bottle could be reused and refilled with any flavor, without first sorting by flavor. The contents were then identified by the crown.

There were many crowns with "root beer" written on them, but no brand name. Different designs and colors provide for a small collection in itself.

Brands represented:

A.D. Simmons	Buck	Donald Duck	Hi Port	Kreemo
A-Treat	Bums	Dr. Mutch's	Hi-Q	Kreger's
A&W	Burkhardt	Dr. Swett's	Hi-Top	Kuntz
Ace	Bybee	Duffy's	High Rock	Kurleys
All American	Calandra	Edelweiss	Hires	Lane's Gold Seal
Anderson's	Canada Dry	Ellwein's	Hoffman	La Vida
Bar-B	Canfield	Fanta	Hollywood	Larue
Barons	Carnation	Farr	Honeymaid	Lasser's
Barqs	Casco	Fawn	Howdy	LC
Barrelhead	Catalina	Faygo	Howels	Leary's
Baumeister	Chey-Rock	Filbert's	Hygrade	Ligonier
Beacon	Circle A	5-Hi	Hydrox	Lincoln
Belfast	Clearock	Fox Springs	IBC	Lithia
Bernicks	Clicquot Club	Frostie	IC	Lord Maxwell's
Bernie's	Cloverdale	Garden City	Indian Club	Love
Big Ben's	Consumer's	Garden State	Indian Queen	Lulu
Big Boy	Cordone's	Gold Coast	Jack Frost	Lyons
Big Chief	Cott	Golden Age	Jack's	M&M
Big Horn	Cragmont	Golden Bridge	Jackson	Ma's
Big Shot	Crass	Golden West	K	Mac's
Bireley's	Crush	Goody	Kasten's	Magnus
Birrell's	Crystal	Grandpa Grafs	Kay-C	Majestic
Blackhawk	Dad's	H&H	Kecks	Manhatten
Blatz	Dana	Hanigan Bros.	Kenwood Club	Mason's
Blenheim	Day's	Happy	Kerns	Maui
Bonnie Maid	Diamant	Health Way	King Bee	McGahan
Botl-O	Diet-Rite	Heep-Good	Kist	Mello
Bottoms Up	Dirigo	Heinie's	Kool Aid	Milton
Brownie	Dodger	Hi Klas	Kravemor	Minnehaha Springs

Mission	O'Neal's	Rock Spring	Sunburst	Virginia Dare
Mohr Bros.	Oneta Club	Rondo	Suncrest	Vogals
Monroe	O-So	Royal	Sunny	Wagner's
Montreal	Ozark Maid	Royal Family	Sunrise	Walt's
Mother's Pride	Pappy's	Royal Flush	Sunspot	Welch's
Mountain Mist	Parade	Sander's	Swallows	West Coast
Mr. Root Beer	Par-T-Pak	Santa Fe Trail	Sweet Sixteen	Whistle
Mrs. Lombardi's	Patio	Schmidt's	Teddy's	White Rock
Mt. Desert	Pequot	Schultz	Ted's	White Rose
Mug	Pic-Nic	Schuylkill	Tiger	Wilson's
My Pop's	Pik-A-Pop	Snowy Peak	Tiny Tim	Windham
Myopia Club	Pop	Solon Springs	Tolls	Windsor
Natco	Pop Shoppe	Sparkeeta	Tom Moore	Wins
National	Purity	Sparkel	Tom Tucker	Wold's
Nehi	Queen-O	Sprecher's	Top Treat	Wolverine
Nesbitt	R	Spurgeon's	Town House	Woosie's
Niagara	Rain-Bo	Squeeze	Towne Club	X
Nodak	Rainbow	Standard	Triple AAA	Yankee Doodle
Nutro	Ramages	Star Bottling Works	Triple XXX	YD
Old Castle Co.	Ramblin'	Star Ice & Soda	Try Me	Yosemite
Old Colony	Rands	Steinberger's	Twang	Yukon Club
Old Jug	Red Arrow	Steven's	UIC	Zetz
Old Newbury	Regent	Stone Jug	U-Zo	Zills
Olliver's	Richardson	Stop & Shop	Vegas Vic	
On Tap	Ritz	Sunbow	Vess	

Bottle crowns, A.D. Simmons to Crass.   Bottle crowns, Crush to Hires.

Bottle crowns, Hires to Manhattan.

Bottle crowns, Mason's to Rainbo.

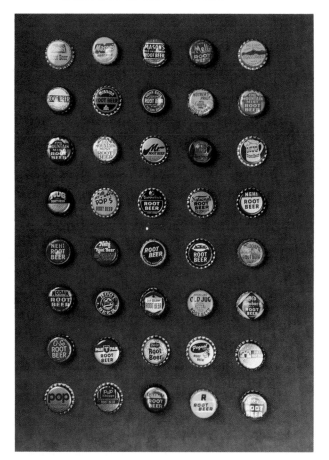

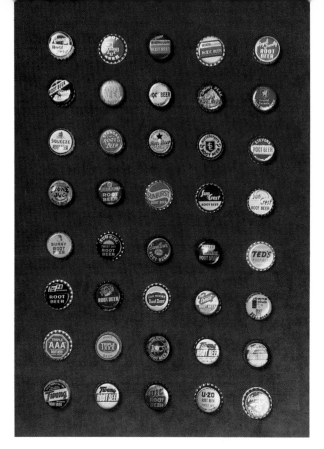

Bottle crowns, Ramages to Vegas Vic.

Bottle crowns, Vess to Yukon Club. Larger crowns are screw-on type for the glass, gallon syrup jugs.

Bottle Openers

When the bottle cap (crown) was invented in 1892, it created the need for a tool to remove it! The bottle opener was invented by none other than he who invented the crown! William Painter of Baltimore, Maryland was granted a patent for his lifter on February 6, 1894.

Hundreds of different types of openers have been created since its creation, limited only to the imagination. Many beverage companies used it to advertise their product, but not to the extent as did the thousands of beer companies. Pepsi, Coke, Dr. Pepper, 7-Up, Royal Crown and Orange Crush are commonly found on numerous types of openers. This is not so with the smaller beverage companies. Their limitation of advertising on openers was certainly in proportion to their size. If a local family operation produced only one flavor, like root beer, the probability of an opener existing for that brand would be unlikely. Of all the root beers, Hires openers would be the most common. Any others would be quite rare.

Brands represented:

A&W	Hires
Barq's	Mason's
Blair's	Minnehaha
Crown	Papoose
Deborah	Quevic
Dr. Swett's	Swallow's
Frostie	

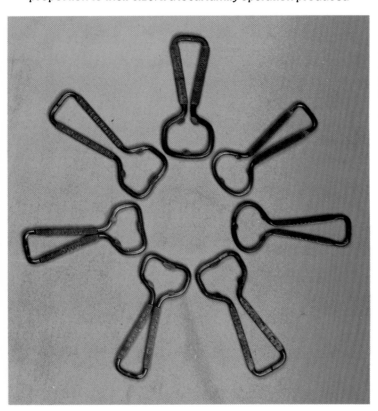

Wire-formed bottle openers, patented in 1915. Clockwise from top: Barq's; Quevic; Deborah; Mason's; Frostie; Hires; and Swallow's.

Bottle openers. Top: Minnehaha, key shaped, patented 1901, length 2¾". Middle: Blair Beverage Co., drink Molto, Blairs root beer, key shaped, patent c. 1901, length 3". Bottom: Crown Bottling Co., Sodas, root & herb beer, figural bottle shaped, patented Mar. 12, 1912, length 3⅛". Has Prest-O-Lite key (the square hole was used as a wrench to open a valve on carbide tanks located on early automobile running boards. These tanks provided gas for the headlights).

Bottle openers. Top: Dr. Swett's, flat metal, 4" in length. Middle: Barq's, over the top style patented in 1924, length 4¼". Bottom: A&W, combination cap lifter/can piercer, c. 1940s, length 4".

Chapter 4
Cans

Can It!

Can a can can a can?
No, a can can't can!
Only you can can.
If I can can and you can can,
How many can we can,
When we can a can?
Can't!
Sure you can can!
Only a can can't can a can!
Can a can can-can?

No, only a can-can can can-can.
Can a can go to the can?
No, you can and I can,
but a can can't.
Why can't it?
It's the same old story—
Some can, some can't,
But a can never can.
—and that's uncanning!

This little jingle refers to canning, such as canning peaches, jams or jellies. Strange how the word originated since canning was done in glass jars!

The first successful can was the steel flat-top, patented by the American Can Company in 1934. In 1935, the cone-top steel can was introduced by the Continental Can Company. It was sealed by a cork crown which required a lift opener to remove it. Popular until the early 1950s, the cone-top can has since become highly collectable. Steel cans had pull tabs in the late 1950s.

The next major change in cans came in 1962 with the appearance of the aluminum can. It was light weight, more economical, and contained its own built-in opener; the pull tab. The pull tab completely disconnected from the can after opening and, in most cases, became part of the ground litter! The pull tab was replaced by the lift tab, which remained attached to the can after opening.

Although the standard size is 12 ounces, cans, like the bottles, may exist within the same brand in variations, generations and different sizes.

Many grocery store chains, local and national, sold root beer at one time or another under their own name/house brand, as did drugstores, discount stores and a hotel or two—Holiday Inn and Howard Johnson's. Many district and regional outlets provided the means for testing the marketability of new root beers prior to a full scale, nationwide launch. Indeed, certain brands had a short life, while others were only popular enough to maintain their limited demand. Still others climbed to national recognition.

Brands represented:

A&P	Baystate	Booth's	Centrella	Crass
A&W	Becker's	Bottoms Up	Certified Red Label	Crystal
Acme	Belfast	BPI	Checkers	Crystal Club
Adirondack	Bells	Braums	Chek	Cue
After the Fall	Berk's County	Brimfull	Chicago Club	Custom
Alaska	Best Choice	British-American	Chug-a-lug	Dad's
Albany Public	Best Yet	Brookdale	Circle K	Daisy
All Star Dairies	Bev-Rich	Buffalo Rock	Click	Dart Drug
Alpha Beta	Big Deal	C&C	Cliquot Club	Del Monte
Always Good	Big 8	C&C Super	Clover Club	Delta
Always Save	Big K	C&C Super Coola	Club House	Diamond Head
American Dry	Big Shot	Camellia	Convenient Food Marts	Diet-Rite
American National	Big Y	Camelot	Co-op	Dis-go
Ann Page	Bi -Lo	Cana	Corr	Dixi
Appletree	Bi-Rite	Canada Dry	Cott	Dlite
Aristocrat	Blue Boy	Can-A-Pop	Cotton Club	Doc's
A-Treat	Blue Sky	Canfield's	Country Club	Donald Duck
Bala Club	Boller	Carnival	Country Fair	Dr. Brown's
Barq's	Bonnie Hubbard	Cascade Pride	Country's Delight	Duchess
Barrelhead	Bon-Ton	Celebrate	Cragmont	Duffy's

Econo Buy
Edwards
Eisner
Elf
Esquire
Fame
Family Dollar
Fanta
Farmview
Faygo
Fay's
Fedmart
Fine Fair
Finast
1st
Fitz
FM
Food & Deli
Food Club
Foodland
Food-Rite
Food Town
Frank's
Frolic
Frostie
Fyne-Time
Galaxy
Gayla
Giant Food
Glendale
Gold Medal
Golden Age
Golden Dawn
Golden Treat
Good Value
Gopher
Grandpa Graf's
Grand Union
Gristedes
Handi
Handy Andy
Hansen's
Happy Time
Harvest Day
Hawaiian Delite
Hep
Hertage House
Hillcrest
Hills
Hi-Q
Hires
Hi Sparkl
Hoffman
Holiday
Holiday Inn
Hollywood
Holy Cow
Home & Garden
Howard Johnson
Howdy
Hyde Park

Hydrox
Hy-Top
Hy-Tyme
Hy-Vee
I.B.C.
Ideal
IGA
Iris
Janet Lee
Jefferson Club
Jewel
Jolly Good
Jolly Pop
Jolly Treat
K&B
Key
Key Food
King Kooler Jr
Kingston
Kirsch
Kist
Klondike
Kohls
Krasdale
Lady Lee
Laurel Spring
Lawson
Lenox Park
Loblaws
London Dry
Lori's
Lotsa
Love
Lucky
Lucky Strike
Mad Butcher
Mark IV
Marsh
Ma's
Mason's
Mavis Club
Mayfair
Mayfresh
Meadowdale
Meijer
Meyers
Mission
Montco
Montreal
Mother's Pride
Mr. Root Beer
Mug
My Pop
Nancy Jane
National
Nehi
Nesbitt's
Newport Club
Nine-O-Five
No-Cal
Norwest

Ol' Smoothie
Old Colony
Old Dutch
Old Time
On-Tap
Ontario
Orchard Park
Our Family
Pabst
Pacemaker
Pantry Pride
Parade
Park
Park Club
Parson's
Par-T-Pak
Party Club
Pathmark
Patio
Peer
Penguin
Peoples
Piggly Wiggly
Pin-Mar
Pioneer
Pix
Plaza
Plus
Pocono
Polar
Pop-O
Price Chopper
Pri-Pak
Provigo
Publix
Purity Supreme
QT
Queen of Scot
Rainbow
Ralph's
Ramblin'
Red & White
Red Owl
Regent
Rex
Richfood
Ritz
Riverside
Rocky Top
Root 66
Rooti
Royal Islands
Royal Palm
SA (Super America)
Salute
Sav-on
Schnuck's
Schweppe's
Scot Lad
Scotch Buy
Scotty

Scramble
Sentry
7-11
'76
Shasta
Shop 'n Bag
Shopper's Value
Shop Rite
Shopwell
Shortstop
Shurfine
Silver Spring
Simpson Springs
Skaggs
Slender
Smash
Smile
Snow Peak
Snowy Peak
Soda Hut
Soda King
Soho
Sparkel
Spartan
Spree
Springfield
Squeeze
Staff
Stars
Stater Bros.
Stayung
Stop & Shop
Stop 'n Go
Suburban
Sunday Funnies
  -Beetle Bailey
  -Blondie
  -Hagar
  -Popeye
Sun-Glo
Sun Glory
Sunny Jim
Sunnyside
Sun-Rise
Sunshine
Super S
Sussex
Sweet Life
Sweet 'n Low
Sweet Valley
Swifty
Tab
Target
Tartan
Taste Well
Taylor Maid
Texas
Thorofare
Thrifty
Ticket
Tico

Ting
Tip Top
Tom Moore
Tom Thumb
Topmost
Top Treat
Topp
Tops in Pops
Tower
Triple
Triple AAA
Triple XXX
Tubz
TV
Twang
Two Guys
Uncle Jake's
Unity
Valu-Check'd
Valu-Time
Valu-Vend
Variety Club
Varsity
Veri
Vess
Vons
Waist Watchers
Waldbaum's
Wawa
Wegman's
Weight Watchers
Weingarten
Weis
Welch's
Western Family
Western Valley
White Rock
White Rose
Wildwood
Yukon
Yukon Club
Yummy
Zesty
Zing

Various brand name cans

Generic cans (no brand names).

Chapter 5
Dispensers

Dispensers were used at soda fountains across the nation during the first half of the twentieth century. They were small enough to be displayed on the back counter behind the fountain, and to catch your eye, were elaborately designed to enhance the brand name and its syrup contained within.

There are basically two types of early dispensers. The pump style allowed the soda jerk to pump the dispenser several times to get as much syrup as needed. Its function was simple. Since the dispenser was hollow, the pump mechanism could be inserted from the top. It had its own stainless steel lid attached at about one-third from its own top and served as a cover for the dispenser opening. When the plunger was pushed down, the syrup was forced up and out of the provided spout. The other type of dispenser was a spigot protruding from the side of the dispenser near the bottom of the syrup bowl. Some were turn-type handles and some were push-release buttons. Either allowed the syrup to flow.

Since neither type could correctly measure the amount of syrup dispensed, early glasses had a syrup line which indicated one ounce. As dispensing became more advanced, the need for a syrup line was no longer required.

The Bardwell's root beer canteen is unique and should be mentioned. It's blue and gray stoneware is shaped like the old canteens used by the Union Calvary way back when! A wooden handle attached by wires allows it to be carried. A cork is used to plug the top opening. One could consider it a picnic jug for personal use.

Brands represented:

Albers	Magnus
Bardwell's	Massey's
Buckeye	Middleby
Dandy	Murray's
Douglas	Rochester
Fowler's	Ruby
Hires	Stearn's

Buckeye syrup dispenser. Porcelain, "Cleveland Fruit Juice Co., Cleveland, Ohio" written on base. 13½" h. Pump type.

Douglas syrup dispenser. Porcelain, 14½" h, pump type.

Buckeye syrup dispenser. Porcelain, tree stump shaped, "Cleveland Fruit Juice Co., Cleveland, Ohio" written on bottom. Pump type, 14¾" h.

Hires toy dispenser, plastic, workable. Holds contents of one bottle of root beer! Flat back, turn-type spigot. 11" x 6¼" x 4¾" deep.

Bardwell's canteen. Shown is a ceramic reproduction, 11¼" h x 9¼" dia. x 4" deep. (Original is stoneware and is larger in size).

Hires syrup dispenser. "The Enduro" was loaned free to dealers who ordered 15 gallons of Hires finished syrup. Adaptable to either counter or back bar by a two foot, long neck stand (not shown). Made of stainless steel, the small emblem on the front states, "accepted by the American Medical Association" to convey that it was not only delicious, but also wholesome! Push-button release. 8½" x 6" x 4", c. 1930s.

Chapter 6
Drinking Glasses

Drinking glasses were used at soda fountains in the drug stores to advertise the store's special brand. The earlier glasses had a syrup line about one inch up from the bottom of the glass. This line aided the soda jerk in measuring the amount of syrup to use before the carbonated water was added. All these are applied-colored labels (ACL).

Brands represented:

A&W	Margo
Challenge	Mason's
Churchill's Aloha	Mrs. Lombardi's
Dad's	Mug
Dr. Swett's	Rochester
Filbert's	Shasta
Hires	Triple AAA

Hires drinking glasses, from left: 5″ h; 5¼″ h; and 4¾″ h.

Drinking glasses, from left: Rochester, 5″ h; Dr Swett's, 4⅜″ h; Mrs. Lombardi's, 4⅝″ h; Filbert's, 4⅜″ h.

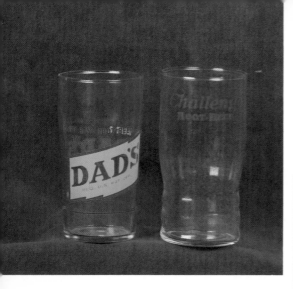

Drinking glasses. Left: Dad's, 4⅞" h. "Don't say root beer, say Dad's" on front. "Have a Dad's black cow ... its delicious" on reverse. Right: Challenge, 5" h.

Drinking glasses, from left: Mug, 6" h; A&W root bear, same picture on reverse, 6¼" h; A&W root bear, "family restaurant" on reverse, 5⅝" h; Mason's, 5⅜" h.

Drinking glasses. Triple AAA, 5¼" h. Shasta, 5½" h.

Margo drinking glass, ACL, syrup line, 4⅜" h, "bonded root beer, aged in wood."

Chapter 7
Magazine Ads

Magazine advertising began to replace the trade card advertising near the beginning of the twentieth century, and was in full swing by the 1920s. As a less expensive method, magazine circulation reached a greater number of people in less time. From full page ads to small corner displays, from color to black and white, root beer companies attempted to convince the public that their product was superior. It appears that only the major root beer companies used the national magazines (*Look*, *Life*, *Saturday Evening Post*) to carry most of their ads. It is interesting to note that the majority of the ads found are by Hires.

Brands represented:

A&W	Hires
Barq's	Richardson
Dad's	

Hires full page magazine ad, 10¼″ x 13¾″, from the July 1928 issue of *Pictorial Review*.

Hires full page magazine ad, 10¼″ x 16″, c. 1897.

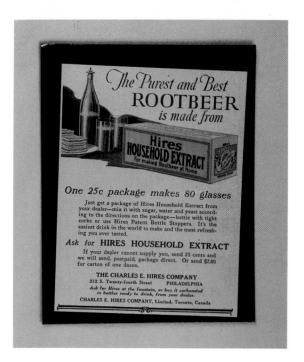

Hires ¼ page ad, 4¾″ x 6¼″, 1922.

Hires full page ad from the July 15, 1933 issue of *Saturday Evening Post.*

Hires full page ad from the June 24, 1933 issue of *Saturday Evening Post.*

Hires full page ad from the September 6, 1937 issue of *Life* magazine.

Hires full page ad from a 1937 issue of *Life* magazine. Many variations exist within this particular basic format, but of different scenes.

Hires full page magazine ad from the June 6, 1936 issue of the *Saturday Evening Post*. Features a cash prize contest for the best reason to drink Hires.

Hires ¼ page ad from the September 15, 1947 issue of *Life* magazine. Many different scenes exist within this basic format for the 1946-1948 issues.

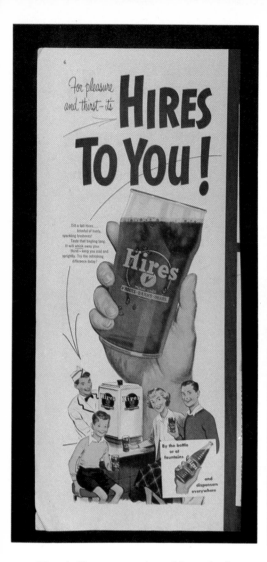

Richardson's root beer, half page magazine ad from the May 16, 1953 issue of the *Saturday Evening Post*.

Hires half page magazine ad from the June 14, 1952 issue of the *Saturday Evening Post*.

A&W root beer full page ad from a 1965 issue of *Look* magazine.

Hires full page ad with Bob Hope from the September 15, 1961 issue of *Life* magazine.

A&W root beer full page ad, featuring Dennis the Menace, from a 1966 issue of *Look* magazine.

Hires full page ad featuring a premium offer for cap liners. *Saturday Evening Post*, April 22, 1967.

Barq's root beer full page ad commending A&W for helping to prove that root beer is a substantial flavor category. *Beverage Industry*, February 1989.

Dad's root beer full page ad in the February 1989 issue of the *Beverage Industry*.

Chapter 8
Matchbook Covers

Matchbooks are an inexpensive form of advertising used by thousands of businesses. The majority are made up from cafes, hotels, restaurants, bars, banks and insurance companies. There are a few soda pops and even fewer root beers.

It is a collector's preference whether the matchbooks should include the matches, but evidence shows that the covers alone seem to be more popular and are certainly easier to display, not to mention safer!

Most matchbooks hold twenty matches (the same number of cigarettes in a pack), but a few can be found containing only ten matches. Di-cut matchbooks are difficult to find.

Brands represented:

A&W	Hires
Barqs	Howel's
Belfast	Old Dutch
Dad's	Reed & Bell
Dr. Swett's	Sparkeeta
Duffy's	Wright

Matchbook covers: Reed & Bell; Dr. Swett's; Howel's; and Wright.

Two Hires matchbook covers.

Tower and Sparkeeta matchbook covers.

Three Dad's matchbook covers.

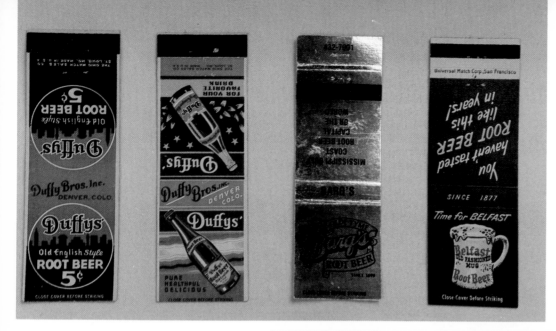

Matchbook covers: Duffy's; Duffy's; Barq's;
Belfast.

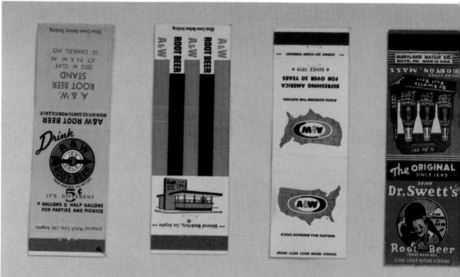

Matchbook covers: Three different A&W's.
Far right: Dr. Swett's.

Matchbook covers: Left: A&W di-cut.
Center: Hires, holds 10 matches rather than
the normal 20. Right: A&W di-cut.

Chapter 9
Mugs

Stoneware (pottery)

Stoneware mugs were predominate in the late 1800s and early 1900s. A few were made of porcelain, ceramic or china and are included in this section.

It was common practice for mugs to be glazed over the letters or design for lasting protection. Sometimes stenciling was applied after the glaze, and with no afforded protection, the markings slowly deteriorated.

Several of the Hires type mugs which display the little boy logo are known as 'Mettlach.' Mettlach is a town in Germany where the Villeroy & Boch stoneware factory was located until it burned down in 1921. Their products included hundreds of now rare steins, each numbered and identified with their logo and the name 'Mettlach.'

Certain mugs, like the Belfast, were given away as a special premium. Others were used over the counter at soda fountains to advertise and serve that special brand.

The Hennessey's is an unusual piece. It appears to be crudely handmade and slightly out-of-round, suggesting a very limited quantity from a very small company. The reference to the "Denver (MUD)" must be an inside company joke—one that may never be known!

Another mystery is the Goose mug. It is unknown whether it is a company symbol or just a design.

The Miner's mug is a very unique piece. The front displays the name on a miner's coal car and the tools of the miner's trade, while the backside shows a miner in the tunnel next to a coal car, swinging a pick.

Brands represented:

A&W	CP (Certified Products)	Graf's	Old Kentucky
American	Croce	Hall & Lyons	Papoose
Armour's Veribest	Dr. Murphy's	Hennessey's	Richardson's Liberty
Barrelhead	Dr. Swett's	Hires	Schuster's
Belfast	Faust	Hunter's	Stearn's
Berry's	GD	Jim Dandy	Stites
Big Top	Gehring's	Kravemor	Triple XXX
Bowey's	Gold Bond	Lash's	Zarembo
Buckeye	Goose design	Miner's	Zipps

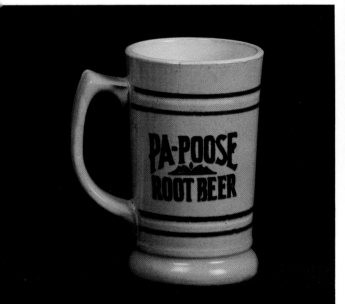

Pa-Poose pottery mug, 5⅜″ h.

Pa-Poose pottery mug, reverse side.

Dr. Swett's pottery mug, 5⅞″ h.

Left: Big Top mug, china, 4½″ h. "Walker China, vitrified Bedford, OH. 1-31″ written on bottom. Right: Stites pottery mug, 5″ h. Top curve of handle contains a king's face with crown.

Berry's salt glaze mug, 4⅛″h.

Hennessey's pottery mug. Appears to be handmade, not glazed, 4½″ h.

"Goose" pottery mug (no brand name), 4¾″ h. A&W 50th Anniversary mug, ceramic, 4″ h, "Florence ceramics Co., a subsidiary of Scripto" written on bottom.

Left: Schuster's pottery mug, 4¾" h. Middle: Triple XXX porcelain mug, 4½" h. Right: Old Kentucky ceramic mug, small picture of man leading a horse, "Hand painted—Japan" written on bottom, 3⅞" h.

Left: Jim Dandy pottery mug, 6¼" h. Center: Belfast Old Fashioned Mug root beer mug, embossed letters, "Tepco China, USA" written on bottom, 4¼" h. Right: Zipps pottery mug, 4⅝" h.

Gehring's pottery mug, 6⅜" h.

Left: Dr. Murphy's pottery mug, 4¼" h. Right: Lash's pottery mug, 6¼" h.

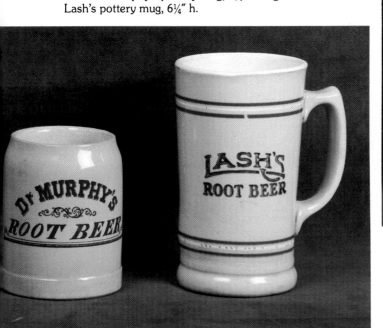

Stearns' pottery mugs, 6⅜" h and 4" h.

Left: Kravemor pottery mug, 4⅞" h. Center:
American pottery mug, 4⅜" h. Right: Graf's
pottery mug, "The Best What Gives," 4¼" h.

Two styles of Buckeye pottery mugs, both
4¾" h. The one on the left is a left-handed
mug.

Left: Buckeye pottery mug, straight sided,
left-handed, 6¼" h. Right: Buckeye, curved
sides, right-handed, 6⅜" h.

Hires pottery mugs. Left: "Hires" in red
letters on reverse, "Cauldon ware, England"
beneath a king's crown logo on bottom, 4″ h.
Right: "Made in Germany for the Charles E.
Hires Company, Villeroy & Boch, Mettlach
#3095," 4″ h, c. 1895.

Hires pottery mugs. 6″ h; 7″ h, "use as
container except for Hires is illegal" written
on bottom! 5½″ h, "Germany" written on
bottom.

Embossed/Etched/Gilded Glass

Embossed—The process of cutting desired letters or designs into the inside surface of the plate mold. Thus, when the liquid glass is poured into the mold, it creates a raised effect which can be felt by running your finger over it.

Etched—The process by which hydrofloric acid is used to burn the desired letters or designs into the glass. It has a frosted-like appearance. The areas not to be etched are covered with acid-resistance substances such as wax, rosin or paraffin.

Gilded—The process of applying gold to the outside of the glass. The letters or designs are painted on the glass with a mixture of gold, pot-ash, and turpentine. During the firing, the turpentine is burned away leaving the gold fused to the glass and producing a flaky appearance.

These expensive methods were used as a means of decoration as well as for advertising. They were quite popular until replaced by the less expensive applied-colored label technique of 1934.

Mugs, of course, are mostly for right handers. This means that when the mug is held in the right hand, the brand name/logo is facing the drinker. Yes, there are some left handed mugs for which the opposite applies. Occasionally the advertisement appears on the common side, opposite the handle, or on both sides, thus accommodating both the left and right hander.

Brands represented:

A&W	Menlo
Bowey's	Richardson's
Dad's	Richardson's Liberty
Fox's	Rochester
Frostie	S&S
Howel's	Stewart's
Lyons	Triple XXX
Magnus	Weber's
Massey's	

Richardson's mugs: Left: Embossed lettering, 5 5/16" h. Right: Etched lettering, 6⅝" h.

Richardson's Liberty mugs, embossed. Left: thick glass and lettering, 4⅝" h. Right: Barrel designed. "Richardson Corporation, Rochester NY" embossed on bottom and only readable from the drinker's point of view! 6⅝"h.

Left: Magnus, gilded lettering, 6⅛″ h. Right: Fox's, etched lettering, 5¼″ h.

A&W embossed mugs. Beaded oval logo, 5¾″ h. Baby mug, block lettering, 3″ h. Standard size, block lettering, heart shaped handle, 4¼″ h.

Left: Frostie, embossed, large outline of elf on backside, 5¾″ h. Center: Bowey's, gilded lettering, 4⅞″ h. Right: Magnus, embossed, 6″ h.

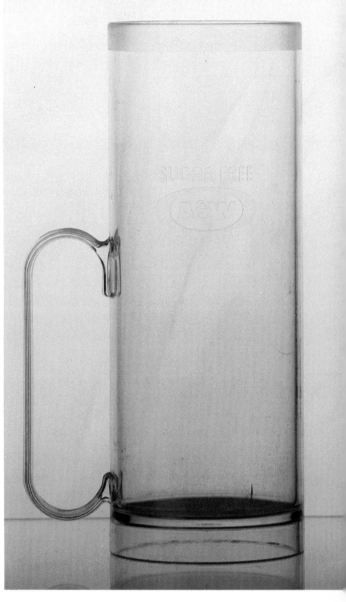

A&W embossed, plastic mug, oval logo, "sugar free," 7¼″ h.

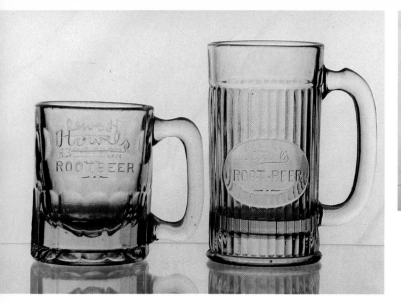

Embossed mugs. Left: Stewart's, beaded lettering, 4½" h. Center: Dad's, barrel designed, 5¼" h. Right: Triple XXX, beaded lettering, 4½" h.

Howel's embossed mugs, two sides on each, 4¼" h and 6" h.

S&S embossed glass mug, 3" h.

Left: Menlo, embossed, "E S CO 4-E-12" on bottom, 5⅜" h. Center: Triple XXX, embossed, white milk glass, 5⅜" h. Right: Lyons, embossed, 6" h. (notice this lyons and the Magnus embossed mug are identical in style and design. See index for further explanation.)

Rochester embossed mugs. Left: flared bottom, 6⅛" h. Right: "J. Hungerford Smith Co., Rochester, NY" readable from the drinker's point of view! 6⅛" h.

Weber's, embossed glass mug, 4¼" h.

ACL Glass

The development of the "applied-colored label (ACL)" technique in 1934 provided a colorful method of applying both advertising and identification not only to soda bottles, but to glass mugs as well. The previous method of embossing was on its way out.

ACL mugs came in three basic sizes: the large (6"), the standard (4½"), and the baby (3"), although other sizes sometimes existed. The 3" baby mug was complimentarily served to the small children. Besides fitting in the tiny hands comfortably, the baby mug contained about the right amount for the tiny one's thirst.

Some of these brands were "drive-in" type restaurants catering to hamburgers, french fries, and cold frosty root beers: A&W; B-K; Dog 'n Suds; Stewart's; and others. Unfortunately, the very localized brands may no longer exist, making research practically impossible. Many of these will remain mysteries of our past culture, but the mug provides evidence that the brands were here. We can admire, enjoy and wonder at its history.

Brands represented:

A&W	Grandpa Graf's	O-So
Auman's	Happy Joe's	On-Tap
B-K	Hires	Park Lane
Barq's	Howel's	Rainbow
Barrelhead	I.B.C.	Ramblin'
Big Ben	Jocko's	Reed & Bell
Challenge	KN	Richardson
Connie	Little Skipper's	Silverfross
Cremel	Lyon's	Stewart's
Dad's	Made Right	TNT
Dog 'n Suds	Menlo	Triple XXX
Frostie	Mugs-Up	Twin Kiss
Frostop	Nesbitt's	Weber's

Various A&W ACL mugs depicting the different logos used. 3" and 6" sizes are shown. Many sizes and variations exist within each logo.

ACLs from left: Auman's, 4½" h; Challenge, 5" h; Barrelhead, 5¼" h; Barq's, 5½" h (a bottle opener for twist-off caps is recessed in the bottom. Also exists without it).

B-K ACL mugs. The four mugs on the left are boxed-logo of various sizes. The three on the right are the criss-cross logo design in various sizes.

Various Dog n Suds ACLs with the original dog picture and the newer sign logo.

Various Frostie's and Frostop's ACL mugs.

ACLs: Howel's, 5¼″ h; I.B.C., 5½″ h; Menlo, 6⅛″ h.

Hires ACLs, "since 1876" within center circle, 3″, 6⅛″, 4½″.

Hires ACLs, 5½″ h, 5⅝″ h, and 3″ respectively.

Hires ACLs, frosted glass, 5⅛″ h, 3″ h ("since 1876" within center circle), and 4½″ h.

ACLs: O-So, 5⅜″ and Jocko's, 4¼″.

KN ACLs: 3″, 4¼″, and 5½″.

ACLs: Lyons, 4¾″ (5″ not shown); Nesbitt's, 5″ (4¾″ not shown); Twin Kiss, 5⅝″ and 3″; Weber's, 5⅜″ and 3″.

ACLs: Mugs-up, logo of a mug pouring onto a drive-in restaurant, 6″ and 4⅜″; Little Skipper's, logo of a mug within a ship's steering wheel, 6″ and 4¼″.

ACLs: Rainbow and Big Ben, both 3″. Existence of other sizes for either brand is not known.

ACLs: TNT, "Loaded with flavor," 4¼″. Park Lane, 4½″. Ramblin', "A product of the Coca-Cola Company," 5¼″. On Tap, (a Pepsico product), 5″.

ACLs: Reed & Bell, 4½″ and 6″. Richardson, 6″ and 4½″.

ACLs: Silverfross, 4¼" and 3" (a 6" exists in addition to the same three sizes in silver lettering). Stewart's, 3" (does not indicate root beer, but "drive-in") and 4½".

Triple XXX ACLs, 5⅜", 5½", and 3".

Plastic ACL mugs. Hi Spark'l, 5⅜". A&W, 6⅝", "Super Sippers" on reverse. Hires, 5⅜" (Digital company logo on reverse) and 5¼". Mug, 5½", logo on both sides.

Chapter 10
Trade Cards

As a means to introduce a business, a service, or a product, trade cards first appeared in the mid-1800s and reached their peak during the turn of the century. They were of different sizes, but averaged 3″ x 5″, and were made of thin card stock. Variations in tones, colors, and printing types for reverse advertisement may exist for the same pictured card. Cards sometimes had the name and address of the local merchant who gave the cards out to the public after receiving them from the company.

Through a new process called chromolithography, the cards became highly colorful and elaborately designed. More times than not, children or animals were featured interacting with the product in some unique fashion. The flip side described the product and its excellent qualities.

By the 1920s, as colored magazine ads were becoming more abundant, the trade card's popularity declined.

It is apparent that Hires produced the greatest amount of trade cards. Other companies were represented, but by their mere size, offered only one or two.

One would surmise that there would be as many brands in trade cards as there are companies who produced extract bottles. After all, at the height of the extract's popularity, trade cards were the most popular and economical method of up-to-date advertising. Unfortunately this doesn't appear to be the case.

Brands represented:

Allen's	Hartshorn's	Taylor's
Bryant's	Hires	Walsh's
Favorite	Knapp's	William's
French's	Raser's	

Hires trade card, 3¾″ x 5¾″, 1883.

Hires trade card, "Paper hat," 3″ x 5″, 1890.

Hires trade cards. Left: "Say Mama," 3″ x 5″, 1891. Right: "Say Mama," 3″ x 4½″, 1892.

Hires trade card, "An Uninvited Guest," 3″ x 5″, 1892.

Hartshorn trade card, 2¾″ x 4½″, c. 1895. Taylor's trade card, 3⅜″ x 5¼″, c. 1895.

Raser's trade card, 3″ x 5″, date unknown.

Hires trade card, 5″ x 6½″, date unknown.

Hires trade card, 5″ x 6½″, date unknown.

Hires trade card, 3¾″ x 5¾″, date unknown.

Hires trade cards: 3″ x 5″, 1897 and 2½″ x 4″, di-cut, 1892.

Hires trade cards. 3″ x 4¾″, 1893. 3⅜″ x 5½″, c. 1895.

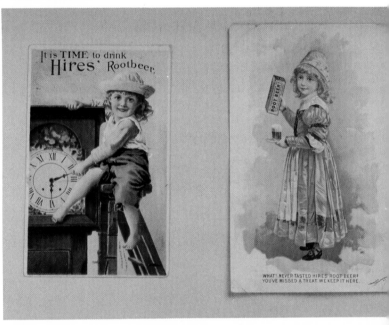

Williams' trade cards. Top: 3″ x 5″, c. 1892 .
Bottom: 3″ x 5″, 1892.

Trade cards. Left: Favorite, 3″ x 5″, c. 1895.
Right: Allen's, 2¾″ x 4⅞″, 1882 (brand name is
on the reverse side, see separate picture).

sample of a trade card's advertising side.
his one is the reverse of the Allen's, 1882,
cturing the child with the bouquet of
wers, dressed in blue.

Allen's trade cards. Left: 2½" x 2½", date
unknown. Right: 3¼" x 5", date unknown.

Knapp's trade card, 2½" x 4⅛", 1893, "Guess
what I got its awful good."

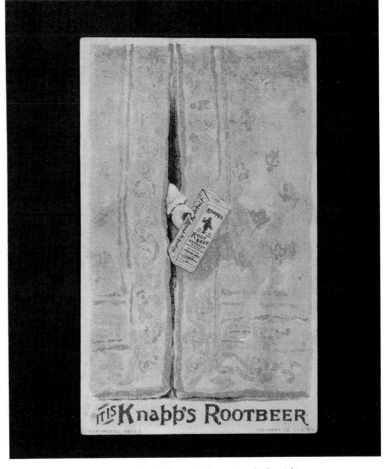

Reverse side of Knapp's featuring little girl in
front of a curtain. Reveals what she had
hidden behind the curtain!

Allen's trade cards. Left: 3¼″ x 4¾″, date unknown. No brand name on front; name and advertising on reverse. Right: 2½″ x 4¼″, date unknown.

Hires trade cards. Left: "His first suspenders", 3″ x 5″, 1896. Right: "All gone", 3″ x 5″, 1894.

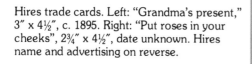

Bryant's trade card, 3½″ x 6″, 1896.

Hires trade cards. Left: "Grandma's present," 3″ x 4½″, c. 1895. Right: "Put roses in your cheeks", 2¾″ x 4½″, date unknown. Hires name and advertising on reverse.

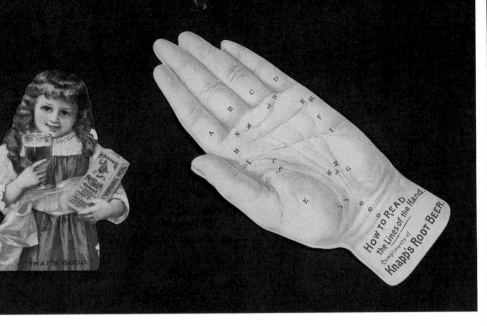

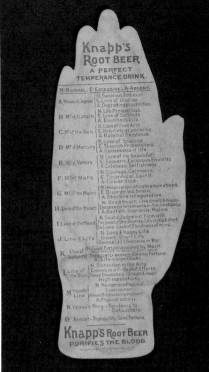

Knapp's trade cards. Left: "That's good!" 2½″ x 3¼″, 1889, di-cut. Right: "Palm reading", 2¼″ x 5¾″, di-cut, 1893, (see reverse picture for letter explanations).

Reverse side of Knapp's "Palm reading." Explains each line in the palm.

Hires trade card, "Ruth and Naomi," 5⅞″ x 5″, date unknown. (see reverse picture for advertising).

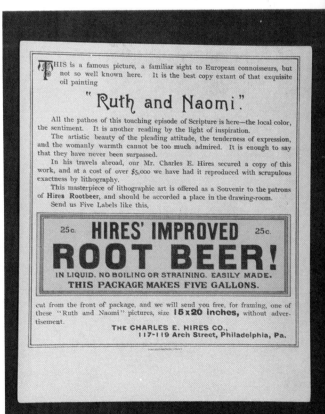

Reverse side of Hires' "Ruth and Naomi."

Hires trade card, "Call back yer dog—call back yer lobster," 2¾″ x 4¼″, date unknown. Appears to be a pencil drawing rather than a lithograph.

Chapter 11
Signs

Signs speak for themselves. Some are square, rectangular, di-cut, self standing (easel type backing for standing or counter display), and multi-colored. They can be found made of tin, porcelain, cardboard, and paper; although those that are paper are normally posters, they will be included with the signs.

Rochester cardboard sign, litho, easel back, 20″ x 21½″, di-cut, "J. Hungerford Smith Co., Rochester, NY."

Clicquot Club cardboard sign, litho, di-cut, easel back, 7″ x 23½″.

Dad's cardboard sign, litho, di-cut, easel back, 10¾" x 16¾".

Dad's cardboard sign, litho, di-cut, easel back, 9¼" x 21¾".

Hires signs, paper, easel back, litho, di-cut. Left: 5⅛" x 6¾", copyrighted 1892. Right: 3⅞" x 5", copyrighted 1897. Back side indicates this to be a small facsimile of a 25 inch high sign available to dealers ordering a gross of Hires root beer.

Kist paper sign, 13½" diameter.

Richardson's tin sign, double sided, hangs from reinforced holes at top, 47" x 59".

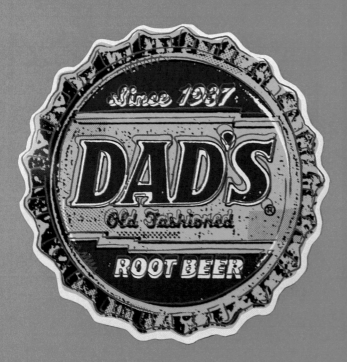

Dad's cardboard sign, 16½" diameter, c. 1989. "Dad's day, July 18" on reverse. These were abundant in certain department stores during the celebration of Father's Day.

Kist cardboard sign, 13" x 20¼".

Mason's tin sign, 9" diameter, cardboard easel back allows for standup or hang up display.

Hires cardboard sign, litho, cut-out, 7¾" x 10¾".

Twang sign, tin, 14¼" diameter.

Polly's cardboard sign, 11" x 13¾", all lettering is recessed.

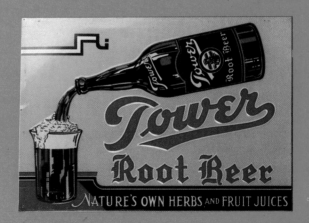

Tower sign, tin, 13¼" x 19¼".

Drink **CANADA DRY**
ROOT BEER
DELICIOUS — REFRESHING

Canada Dry sign, tin, 7″ x 24″.

Norka sign, tin, 12″ x 24″.

NORKA
Root Beer
tastes better

kids love **Ma's** ROOT BEER

Ma's sign, tin, 27½″ x 9½″.

Mason's sign, tin, 12″ x
30″, Stout Sign Co., St.
Louis, MO.

Mason's ROOT BEER
Foam-topped...Refreshing

Hires sign, tin, 11¾" x 29¾".

Goody sign, tin, 13½" x 19½", copyright 1940, American Art Works Inc., Coshocton, Ohio.

Triple AAA tin sign, di-cut, 12¼" x 44", Stout Sign Co., St Louis, MO.

Hires cardboard sign, 3-dimensional, stand-up, 22" x 29¾", copyrighted 1914.

Nehi sign, tin, 11¾" x 29½", "Good
Housekeeping seal of approval," The
Donaldson Art Sign Co., Covington, KY.

Dad's sign, tin, self-framed, 13½" x 29".

Hires sign, tin, 19½" x 27½".

Hires sign, tin, 23¼" diameter.

Mason's sign, tin, 23½" diameter, Stout Sign Co., St Louis, MO.

Hires sign, cardboard, easel back, 18" x 24".

Richardson's sign, tin, self-framed, 22" x 34".
An identical sign, 9½" x 14", exists.

Triple AAA tin sign, self-framed, 19¾" x 27¾", Press Sign Co., St Louis, MO.

Triple AAA sign, tin, self-framed, 19¾" x 27¾", Stout Sign Co., St Louis, MO.

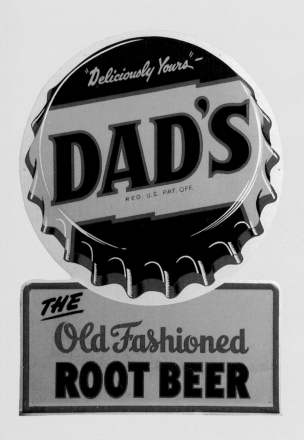

Dad's sign, tin, 20" x 28".

Uncle Dan's sign, tin, 9" x 23¾". Courtesy of David and Kathy Nader.

Hires cardboard sign, di-cut, litho, 6½" x 9¼". A corner advertising piece—folds down the middle to form right angles to each other. Notice the hands would remain touching when folded, c. 1900.

Hires cardboard sign, display type, litho, 35" x 23".

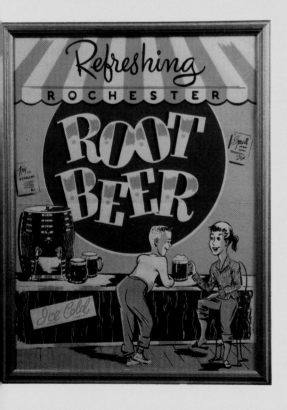

Dad's tin sign, self-framed, 17¼" x 46½". Other sizes of the same design exist.

Rochester paper poster, 18" x 23½".

Hires, store window display, paper, 18″ x 24″.

Top: Golden Bridge tin sign, 3¾″ x 11¾″. Could be a door push plate. Bottom: Richardson tin sign, ¾″ x 12″.

Pilsen cardboard sign, 10¾″ x 18½″, c. 1930.

Triple AAA cardboard sign, 7″ x 13½″.

Richardson paper poster, 11" x 21".

Hires cardboard sign, 19" x 25", c. 1900. Notice the subtle advertising of Hires on the hand-held mugs. Courtesy of John and Marian Swartz.

Hires store display, paper, 11" x 14".

Dub-L-Valu sign, tin, 11⅛" x 18½", Donaldson Art Sign Co., Lovington, KY, 11-27-40. Courtesy of David and Kathy Nader.

Chapter 12
Miscellaneous

Advertising has been presented to the public through many innovative ideas. The methods and items utilized are sometimes quite impressive. Root beer is no exception and advertisements can be found in toys, tokens, postcards, rulers, pinbacks, stuffed animals, ashtrays, pencils, records and much, much more.

Barq's thermometer, tin, 10″ x 25¾″.

Hires thermometer, tin, di-cut, 8″ x 28½″.

Mason's thermometer, tin, 4¾″ x 15¾″.

Hires thermometer, glass face cover, 12″ diameter.

Mason's clock, glass face cover, electric, lighted, manufactured by the Pam Clock Corp., 15½″ x 15½″.

A&W root bear clock, battery powered, 8″ x 12″.

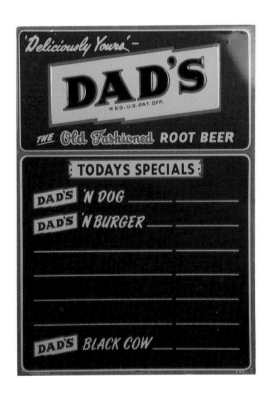

Dad's menu board, tin, 19½″ x 27½″.

Old Frontier clock, plastic, electric, lighted, 12″ x 24¼″.

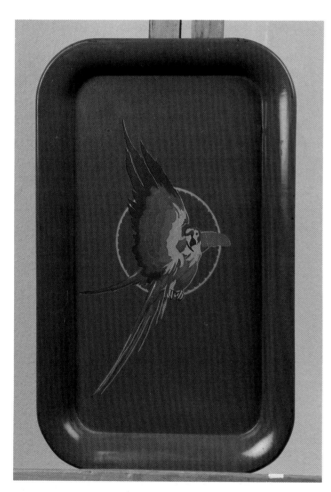

I.B.C. counter top sign, electric, lighted, plastic. Bracket on bottom allows sign to fit counter edge. 6″ x 9″.

Hires tray, tin, 8¾″ x 14⅛″. Hires "bullseye" logo is on reverse. The majority of these trays exist without the Hires logo.

Hires calendar, 1893, 6⅝″ x 7″. The tear-off calendar sheets attached to the bottom are missing.

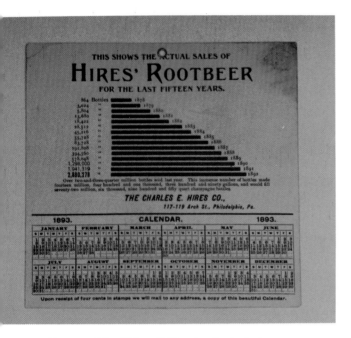

Reverse side of Hires 1893 calendar featuring two children with a kitten.

Hires calendar, 13″ x 13¾″, paper, top portion only, post-1961. (Hires is a registered trademark of Crush International Inc.)

Hires calendar, 1976, 7″ x 11″. ("Hires is a registered trademark of Crush International Inc.")

Hires door push/pull, tin, 2½″ x 13½″.

Triple XXX door push/pull, porcelain, 4¼″ x 34½″.

A&W can lamp, 13½″ h, probably homemade.

Hires decorative mirror, 14¾″ x 19″.

A&W Root Bear pitcher, 8¼″ h, with matching glass, 6¼″ h.

Hires bottle neck advertisement, cardboard, 8¾″ x 11″.

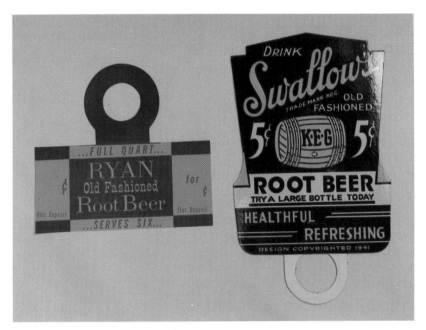

Bottle neck advertisements. Ryan's: card stock, 5″ x 5½″. Swallow's: Coated cardboard, 5″ x 8¼″, design copyrighted 1941.

Dad's bottle neck advertisement, cardboard, 8½″ x 12″.

A&W Root Bears, stuffed, 12½″ small and 32½″ large.

Dad's Root Bear, stuffed, 8¼″, 1985.

Sky High wooden case. Holds six of the half gallon bottle shown. 12″ x 12½″ x 19″.

Different brands of bottle cases. The Hires case is made of thick plastic, the other two of wood. Only the Dad's has individual compartments to hold six "Mama" size amber quarts.

Buckeye wooden barrel dispenser, 27″ h x 14¼″ diameter (measured at top.) Inside are the tubes, hookups and compartments for the syrup, carbonation and refrigeration.

Hires paper cup, 4⅛″, c. 1950s.

Miniature bottles. **Hires**: ACL, 3⅝″ h, a souvenir from the 1948 National Soft Drink Association (NSDA) convention. **Pep-Ade**: Imitation root beer beverage bass, paper label, 3½″ h, "sufficient for twenty glasses of refreshing soft drink." **Dad's**: ACL, 3″ h, boy winking. The existence of a "Papa" and "Mama" size miniature has been reported, but unsubstantiated. **Frostie**: Paper label, 3″ h.

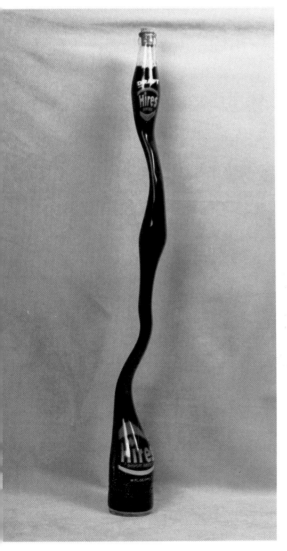

Hires stretch bottle, ACL, 27″ h. Stretch bottles were given as prizes at carnivals and fairs, and most major soda brands were well represented, although the average length was only half this size. The life span of the stretch bottle is normally very short!

Several A&W glass mugs utilized as candle holders.

String hangers made of very light cardboard or paper stock which hung from the ceiling or ceiling fixture by string. They flutter or turn from the slightest wind. **Frostie**: double sided, 5¼". **Hires**: one sided, 11". Could have doubled as a wall decoration. **Dad's**: double sided, 8".

A&W drive-in car window tray, metal, 11" x 14". A&W arrow logo engraved near center.

Paper decals. Triple AAA, 6" x 8". Triple XXX, 6¾" x 8".

Top: Hires ruler, 12", tin, c. 1940s. Bottom: Triple XXX ruler, 12", wooden, c. 1950s.

Hires plastic inflatable cow. 41" l. x 22" h. x
12" w. Can also be hung freely from back
loop.

Hires bottle carrier, cardboard, 8 pak. (Pak 'n
a Pair" was a limited Hires promotion.)

A&W plastic inflatable mug. 49" h x 19½"
diameter, at bottom.

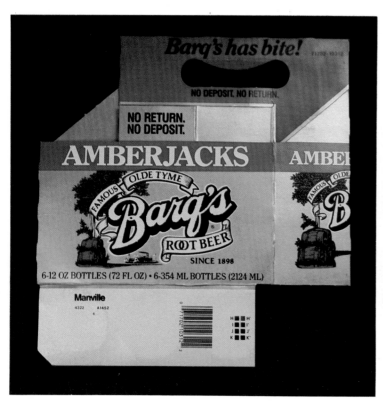

Barq's Amberjacks bottle carrier, cardboard, standard 6 pack.

Hires pocket size mirrors, 2⅛" x 3¼".

Barq's bottle carrier, cardboard, standard 6 pack.

Various 2½" refrigerator magnets.

Belt buckles. A&W, metal, 3¼". Hires, metal, 2⅝" diameter, post-1961 engraved, "Hires is a registered trademark of Crush International Inc., Evanston, IL."

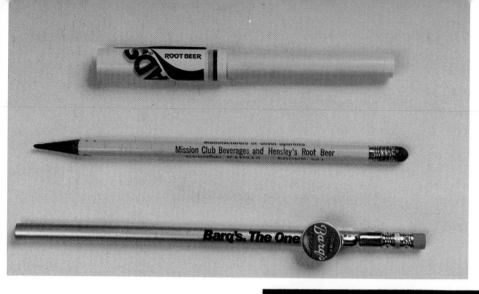

Top: Dad's ballpoint pen, 5½". Center: Hensley's pencil, c. 1940s (bears a 3-digit Newton, Kansas phone number). Bottom: Barq's pencil with attached pocket clip, c. 1989.

Pinbacks. Clockwise from top: A&W, plastic, ½" x 1"; Hires, tin, 2¼" diameter; Dad's, tin, 1⅛" diameter; Hires, tin, 1¾" diameter; Mr. Root Beer, tin, 2¼" diameter.

Tokens. Clockwise from top: **Dad's** bottle cap crimped with a penny inserted in back; **Mason's**, aluminum, 1¼" diameter, "This coin good for one 6 bottle carton of Mason's old fashioned root beer" on front. On reverse, "Dealers this coin will be redeemed by your local mason bottles for 25¢, good only on purchase of Mason's root beer;" **Hires**, tin, 1½" diameter, Hires bullseye logo on reverse; **Lone Star**, wooden, 1½" diameter, "World famous Buckhorn saloon & museum, one free root beer redeemable only at Lone Star Brewery." "Good for one free Lone Star root beer, Lone Star Brewing Co." on reverse; **Jack & Bob's**, wooden, 1½" diameter, "Jack & Bob's drive-in" on reverse; **Cre-Mel**, wooden, 1¼" diameter. Center: **Rochester**, 1½" diameter, brass, root beer contest coin.

Patches. Frostie, 7″ diameter. Hires, 3¾″. Dad's, 2″ x 4″.

Hires 3-note whistle, plastic, horn shaped, 5⅛″ long, inscribed "Drink Hires, it tastes so good" on sides and "Toot for Hires" around outer rim. RARE.

One gallon fountain syrup cans, 8¾″ h.

Simmons & Hammond's pottery syrup jug, one gallon, 12″ h, provides directions for making beer: "Mix contents of this jug with nine gallons of water, put into a soda tank and charge to 125 pounds," c. 1930s.

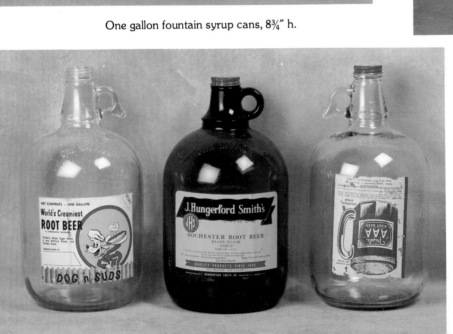

One gallon syrup containers, paper labels. Most of the time the contents were emptied all at once into the dispensing unit. Occasionally, the jug was set into the dispensing unit upside down and slowly drained as it was used, as evident by the Triple AAA jug. The label was right side up when the jug sat upside down.

A&W one gallon syrup jugs, paper labels.

Ramblin one gallon syrup jug, plastic, c. 1980s.

A&W children's lunch box, plastic, 5″ x 8″.

Dad's five gallon syrup container, tin, 13½″ h.

Paper hats. Hires, 4″ x 11″, c. 1940s.
Stewart's, 5½″ x 11¼″, c. 1980s.

Record and sleeve, 331/3 rpm, "Vic Damone Swings with A&W."

Wax cones. Held 32 oz of ready-to-drink root beer. Normally purchased and filled on the spot to take home and refrigerate. One instruction states "Keep chilled and serve within 4 to 6 hours after purchase." 9⅝" high, they are made of coated wax. A metal snap-in, snap-out disc was used for the top enclosure. Once emptied, and the bottoms cut out, they made great megaphones!

Marbles, "Compliments of Tower Root-Beer." A promotional giveaway obtained by the purchase of the brand item. Normally, complimentary premiums are identified by a large hole so that they can be hung around the bottle neck. The premium is usually in the form of a toy to attract a child's attention.

Right:
Helio Jet toy, given away free with the purchase of a carton of Dad's root beer. The large hole allows the premium to hang from the bottle neck and attract a child's attention.

Far right:
A&W take-home jug. Purchased at A&W drive-ins, full, for $1.98, c. 1960s. They could be returned for refills. Tin outer shell, with a glass jug inside. Plastic screw-off top with pour spout and latch. Metal handle. 8¼" h x 6" diameter.

From left: Shasta can bank; Reed's root beer flavored lifesavers; Barrelhead can radio.

Hires postcard, "Alice," 3½" x 5½", 1912.

Cigar box, wood lined, leather covered. 6" x 10¼", made in Spain. Silver plate on top states "With the compliments of DAD'S root beer." May have been given as a gift to recognize certain outstanding salesmen or directors.

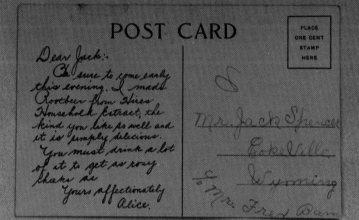

Reverse of Hires "Alice" postcard. Notice the preprinted message from Alice.

Top view of Dad's cigar box.

Left: I.B.C. coaster, cardboard, double-sided, 3⅜″ square. Right: I.B.C. paperweight, glass, 8-sided, 1⅜″ high x 3¾″ diameter.

Dr. Swett's postcard. 3½″ x 5½″. Date unknown. Reverse displays regular postcard form.

Bottle cappers. Aided the home root beer maker in capping the bottles that were filled. Designed to apply the Painter's crown (bottle cap) to one soda bottle at a time, by crimping. Left: Required two hands moving handles outward and downward, causing pinchers to rise and crimp cap into place. Marked on both sides, "Comstock-Bolton Co., Kansas City, MO, U.S.A., pat. 12-21-20." 4″ x 7¼″. Right: Stand type. Could be adjusted for various bottle heights. 15½″ h, metal. No manufacturer's markings (There have been unconfirmed reports that a Hires, with advertising, does exist).

Rochester emblem, aluminum, 6″ x 7½″. (May hang off the side of a dispenser or barrel).

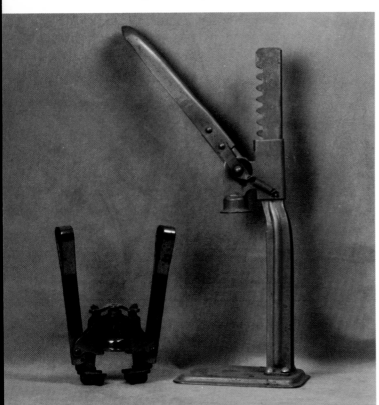

Hires emblem, aluminum, 6″ x 7¾″. (May hang off the side of a dispenser or barrel).

American root beer emblem, pot metal, 2" x 2½", "The American root beer and supply co. makers, Denver. Colo." (may hang off of a dispenser, a barrel, or a bottle case).

Hires cash register top. A decorative, solid brass stand which sits on the top of a cash register. "Fountain Service" on reverse. 3½" x 9". The one pictured is believed to be a reproduction.

A&W hand puppet, cloth, 11" h. A&W frisbee, 9" diameter.

Top: Click root beer clicker, tin, "Drink a Click root beer, the root brew, be a winner," 2½" long. Center: Hires pocket knife, one blade, 3½" long (closed), celluloid handle. Bottom: A&W redeemable coupon for root beer, c. 1950s. (notice the wax cone container).

Richardson barrel emblem, aluminum, curved, 8½" x 11½".

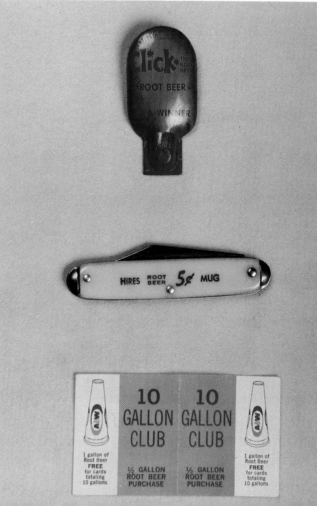

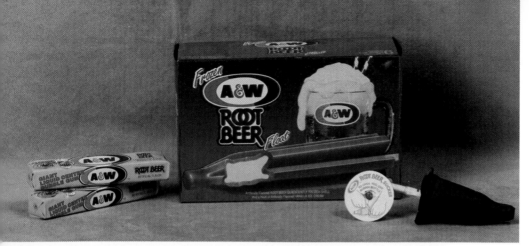

A&W treats. Left: Liquid center bubble gum, first appeared c. 1982. Center: Frozen float on a stick, box of six, c. 1988. Right: A&W root beer sucker. Instructions say "to open, peel off rubber bottle." Cardboard disc sits at bottom of sucker on stick to act as a drip stopper, c. 1987.

Below:
Left: Hires rubber ball, "Drink Hires", 2" diameter. Right: Cloth bag full of bottle caps, 5" x 8½".

From left: A&W key chain, stuffed plastic, 2½" h x 2" w x 1" d. Printer's block of current A&W logo, print face is 9/16" x 17/16". Regulation size golf ball with A&W logo. A&W Chug-a Can II candy container, plastic with paper label, distributed by Fleercorp, Philadelphia. Designed to resemble a military cargo barrel and a play on military jargon—A.W.O.L (absent without leave). "Pure fun...just a joke" on side panel. 2" h x 13/16" diameter.

Vender's apron, 15" x 21", c. 1980s.

Claey's root beer flavored candy.

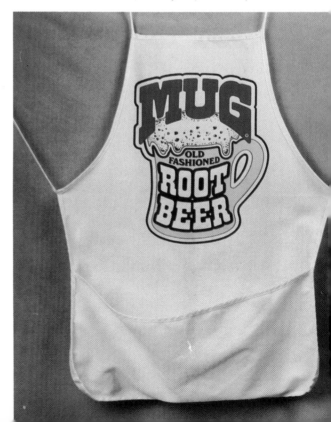

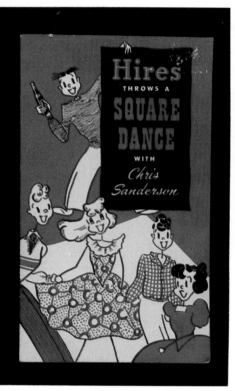

Hires "Square Dance" booklet. 16 pages of pictures, illustrations, and instructions about basic square dancing for the beginner. 4¾" x 7⅞", 1950.

Left: A booklet of recipes made with Hires extracts. Contains instructions in eight different languages. Booklet folds outward as 6 panels, double sided. 3" x 4". Right: Hires booklet, 20 pages, "The legend of the Golden Chair," 3½" x 5", 1895. The story line was about a king who offered his golden chair to any peasant who brought the best new drink for his thirst. The story is also in verse form.

Hires booklet, "The Enchanted Book," 10 pages, 4¾" x 6½". The story line was about a little girl who ventured into an enchanted forest, meeting different characters, and sampling a drink that tastes the same as what her mother gives her.

Hires bottle stopper. Metal screw-down forces flange into lower, hard rubber portion causing expansion and sealing of bottle neck opening. "Hires root beer" embossed in top section of metal. 1¾" x 2¼" average.

Hires flyer featuring barbecue favorites using Hires. Paper, 2⅜" x 8¾". Endorsed by Bob Hope, c. 1950s.

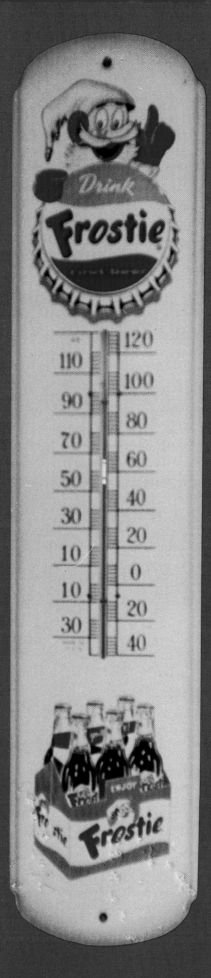

Schuster's thimble, ceramic, 1¼" h. x 1" dia. at base. Pictures a couple sharing a root beer with two straws. Courtesy of David and Kathy Nader.

Dr. Swett's match safe, metal, embossed picture of a dispenser, 2⅝" x 1⅞" x 9/16". Courtesy of David and Kathy Nader.

Frostie's thermometer, tin, 7" x 38".

Standard root beer barrel, wooden, brass banding. Lid is wooden with brass rim attached to top side, providing a tray-like appearance. 25" high, 15" diameter. Cooling unit inside. Three brass 1" scroll-type legs support the barrel. Courtesy of John and Marian Swartz.

A listing of brand names

Besides an alphabetical listing of the 831 root beer brands that I am able to presently substantiate, this listing serves as an index. It also functions as a reference of additional information not mentioned elsewhere.

In many instances, the item itself is the only available source of information. The locations cited were taken directly from the advertising piece, if provided, and may or may not be conclusive as the place of origin. They may differ with each item of the same brand and could be just a bottling, canning, or distribution site. With more cross representation of the brand, further pinpointing may be possible.

It is virtually impossible, and probably irrelevant, to determine when a company, if applicable, added root beer to their line of flavors. When an approximate date is shown (i.e. c. 1974), this merely indicates that the brand existed at that time although the inclusive dates remain unknown.

It may be possible to estimate a brand's span of time by the type of items the company used for advertising. Indeed, as more are discovered and more information is gathered, each brand's time frame may become better defined.

A.D. Simmon's—Denver, CO—37, 38

A&P—A&P Grocers, Montvale, NJ—41, 43

A-Treat—A Treat Bottling Co., Allentown, PA 37, 38, 41, 43

A&W—Started in Lodi, CA in 1919 by Roy Allen and Frank Wright. The initials of their last names formed the company name. One of their first four outlets featured tray boys for curb service, which may well have been the country's first drive-in restaurant! During its peak period in the early 1960s, A&W drive-ins totaled over 2500 franchised outlets. By the early 1980s, the total had decreased to around 500. In the late 1970s, after many takeovers, buyouts, etc, A&W emerged as two separate companies. A&W Brands, Inc. handles the cans and bottles, and A&W Restaurants, Inc. continues to serve root beer on tap.
The J. Hungerford Smith Co., Rochester, NY (who also produced their own brand of root beer—Rochester) made the root beer concentrate for A&W since A&W's beginning in 1919. They bought A&W in 1963, and in turn, both were bought by United Fruit Company in 1966. Some interesting notes: A&W was available in bottles in 1971. Sugar Free A&W began in 1974. The "Root Bear" logo appeared circa 1976. A&W bought Squirt Beverages in 1986. Pepsi Cola bottling became A&W's sole distributors in 1986. Four logos have been used: Circle with arrow, "ice cold" 1919. Circle with arrow, no "ice cold" 1924. A&W in double oval in USA map 1973 A&W within double oval 1975.—8, 12, 14, 23, 24, 37, 38, 40, 41, 43, 55, 56, 57, 60, 61, 62, 64, 65, 66, 70, 71, 73, 78, 102, 103, 105, 106, 107, 108, 109, 111, 112, 115, 116

Ace—California, circa 1945—37

Acme—41

Adams—distributed in Wisconsin and Pennsylvania circa 1954—23

Adirondack—Adirondack Beverage Co., Scotia, New York—41, 43

After the Fall—After the Fall Inc., Brattleboro, Vermont—41, 43

Alaska—Alaska Beverage Co., Fairbanks, Alaska—41

Albany Public—41

Albers—53

All American—California Beverage Co., Chicago, Illinois, c. 1944—37, 38

All Star Dairies—41

Allen's—An extract "prepared only by C.E. Carter-Pharmacist, Lowell, Mass."—9, 79, 82, 83, 84

Aloha—(see Churchill's)

Alpha Beta—Alpha Beta Co., La Habra, CA—41, 43

Always Good—Assoc Wholesale Grocers, Kansas City, KS—41, 43

Always Save—Assoc Wholesale Grocers, Kansas City, KS—41, 43

American—American Root Beer & Supply Co., 1027 Larimer, Denver, CO. The company is listed in the 1907-1914 Denver Directory as "manufacturer of iceless soda fountains, steam tables, and cafeteria work. phone Main #162. Erhard Menig—President".—65, 68, 115

American Dry—41

American National—American National Beverage Division, Mission of California, New Haven, Connecticut—41, 43

Anderson's—New York circa 1947-70.—37, 38

Anheuser-Busch—The famous "Budweiser" Co., St. Louis, Missouri—14, 15

Ann Page—A&P Grocer's, Montvale, NJ—41, 43

Appletree—Appletree Markets Inc., Houston, TX—41, 43

Aristocrat—Wharton Beverage Packers, Wharton, TX—41, 43

Armour's Veribest—65

Auman's—73

Aunt Wicks—Jelsert Co., Chicago, IL

Ayd's—Joseph Ayd, Baltimore, MD—9

B/K—A drive-in type restaurant, originated in Michigan City, Indiana, c. 1946, by "Bergie" Bergarson and Bill Kenefick. The initials of their last names formed the company name. This small company is not to be confused with Burger King, the national hamburger franchise of today. The B/K employed car hops and catered to root beer, sandwiches and such. It was a franchise which supplied syrup, paper, etc., directly to site locations. Each site displayed the logo and the buildings were uniformly painted orange and cream color. The outlets were concentrated in the Indiana, Ohio and Michigan area. However, in 1955, Mr. William H. Vickers opened the first of four B/K drive-ins in Pueblo, CO. As of 1988, Mr. Vickers was still residing in Pueblo and said that the last remaining B/K in Pueblo burned down in 1969. According to Mr. Don Mcnutt of the Denovo Co. in Utica, Michigan, as of August 1987, fifty-seven B/K drive-ins were still operating in the three state area previously mentioned. The Devono Company, as of 1987, owned Tasty Freeze, Dairy Isle, Dog'n Suds, and B/K.—23, 73

Baker's—Baker Extract Company, Springfield, MA. Produced an extract called Baker's Indian Root Beer Extract.—9, 10, 23, 24

Bala Club—Acme Markets Inc., Philadelphia, PA—41, 43

Bar-B—Quality Beverage Co., Los Angeles, CA—37

Bardwell's—53, 54

Baron's—Dinelle Ent., Chico, CA, c. 1971—37

Barq's—Started in Biloxi, Mississippi in 1898 by Edward Barq. First bottled by Biloxi Artesian Bottling Works. Today it is located in New Orleans and is supervised by Edward "Sunny" Barq IV, and has become one of the major brands. The latest slogan is "The one with the bite."—12, 13, 23, 24, 37, 38, 40, 41, 43, 57, 61, 62, 64, 73, 98, 108, 109

Barrelhead—a product of Canada Dry Corp, Maywood, IL, c. 1977—23, 24, 37, 38, 41, 43, 65, 73, 113

Baumeister—Kewaunee Orange-crush Bottling Co., Kewaunee, WI—37, 38

Baystate—41

Beacon—Massachusetts, c. 1950—37

Bean's—9

Becker's—41

Belfast—San Francisco, CA, c. 1930s. Was advertised as "Belfast Mug Root Beer." Sometime in the late 1950s, the "Belfast" was dropped and the company continued as the "MUG" Co. Today it is owned by Pepsi-Cola.—14, 23, 25, 31, 37, 38, 41, 43, 62, 64, 65, 67

Bell's—Bells Markets Inc., Buffalo, New York—41, 43

Berk's County—(A NEHI product). North-South Beverage, Charlotte, NC—41, 43

Bernick's—Chas A. Bernick Inc., St Cloud, MN—37

Bernie's—37, 38

Berry's—65, 66

Best Choice—Assoc Wholesale Grocers Inc., Kansas City, KS—41, 43

Best Yet—Food Brands Inc., Concordia, KS—41, 43

Bev-Rich—Bev-Rich Products Inc., Philadelphia, PA—41, 43

Big Ben—37, 73, 77

Big Boy—37, 38

Big Chief—37, 38

Big Deal—Alfred M. Lewis Inc., Riverside, CA—41, 43

Big 8—Big 8 Stores Advertising Group Inc., El Paso, TX—41, 43

Big Horn—37, 38

Big K—Kroger Co., Cincinnati, OH—41, 43

Big Shot—Jefferson Bottling Co., (Pailet Indust). Metairie, LA—37, 41, 43

Big Top—65, 66

Big Y—Springfield, MA—41

Bi-Lo—Bi-Lo Inc., Mauldin, SC—41, 43

Bireley's—37, 38

Bi-Rite—41

Birrell's—Birrell's Bottling Co., Salt Lake City & Provo, Utah—37, 38

Black Bear—Black Bear Beverages, Inc., St. Francis, WI—14, 23

Blackhawk—Carse & Ohlweiler Co., Rock Island, IL—14, 20, 37

Blackler, J.H.—Westerly, RI (old wooden crate exists)

Blair—Blair Beverage Company—40

Blanchard's—Blanchard Bottling Works, Kaplan, LA—23, 25

Blatz—Blatz Brewing Co., Milwaukee, WI—37

Blenheim—Blenheim Corp, Blenheim, SC—37, 38

Blue Boy—Curtice-Burns Foods Inc., Rochester, NY—41, 43

Blue Sky—Blue Sky Natural Bev. Co., Santa Fe, NM—41, 43

Bobby's—Silver Springs Co., Madison, WI—14

Boller—41

Boulevard—Boulevard Beverage Co., Los Angeles, CA—14, 18

Bonnie Hubbard—United Grocers Ltd., Richmond, CA—41, 43

Bonnie Maid—Napa Rock Bottling Works, CA—37, 38

Bon-Ton—41

Booth's—41

Botl-O—37, 38

Bottoms Up—37, 41

Bowey's—65, 70, 71

Boyd & Beard—11

BPI—Distributed by Beverage Packing Inc., Fort Worth, TX—41, 51

Braum's—Canned under auth of Braum's Ice Cream Co., Oklahoma City, OK., by Oklahoma Bev Co., Okmulgee, OK—41, 43

Brillion—Brillion Bottling Co., Crillion, WI—14

Brimfull—Red Owl Stores Inc., Hopkins, MN—41, 43

British American—British American Operation, Hudson, NY—41, 43

Brookdale—41

Brownie—Bottled by Atlas Bottling Co., Detroit, MI—23, 25, 37, 38

Bruce's—Pure Natural Waters Co., Pittsburgh, PA—14

Bryant's—Williams, Davis & Brooks & Co., Detroit, MI—9, 10, 79, 84

Buck—37

Buckeye—Cleveland, OH—53, 54, 65, 68, 104

Buffalo Rock—41

Bulls Eye—Bottled by Squirt Bottling Co., Grand Island, NE—23, 25

Bum's—K's Beverages Co., Los Angeles, CA c. 1941—23, 25, 37, 38

Burkhardt—Illinois c. 1958—37, 38

Burrough—Burrough Bros. Mfg. Co., Baltimore, MD. Chemists since 1863—9

Burton's—9

Bybee—Bybee Bottling Works, Vancouver, WA—37

C&C—C&C Cola, Elizabeth, NJ—41, 44

C&C Super—Cantrell & Cochrane Corp., New York, NY—41, 44

C&C Super Coola—Cantrell & Cochrane Corp., New York, NY. 9 flavors introduced in 1953 all in 6 or 12 oz cone-top cans.—41, 44

Calandry—37

Camellia—41

Camelot—C&M Marketing Co., Detroit, MI—41, 44

Campbellsport—Campbellsport Bottling Works—14, 21

Cana—Great Lakes Canning Inc., Twinsburg, OH—41, 44

Canada Dry—Originated in Toronto, Canada, c. 1907. Original logo was a beaver within map of North American with king's crown above. Beaver was later dropped. Presently a division of Beatrice Foods, Chicago.—37, 38, 41, 44, 90

Can-a-Pop—S&C Sales Co., Denver, CO—41, 44

Canfield's—A.J. Canfield Co., Chicago, IL—37, 38, 41, 44

Carnation—Carnation Bottling Co., Mt Vernon, MO—23, 25, 37

Carnival—Weis Markets Inc., Sunbury, PA—41, 44

Cascade Pride—Three J's Dist Inc., Milwaukee, OR—41, 44

Casco—37

Catalina—37

Celebrate—41

Centrella—Central Grocers Coop., Franklin Park, Illinois—41, 44

Certified Red Label—41

Challenge—55, 56, 73

Champion—Finnerty, McClure & Co., Philadelphia, PA—9

Chek—Deep South Products Inc., Orlando, Florida. Distributed through Winn-Dixie Supermarkets.—41, 44

Checkers—Interstate Canning Co., Louisville, KY—41, 44

Chey-Rock—In 1910, the Mobridge Carbonating Company, in Mobridge, South Dakota opened. Its limited distribution serviced the surrounding counties. The Mobridge area was nationally famous for an early resident who is now buried there—Tantanka Iyotake, better known as Chief Sitting Bull, the victor over General Custer at the battle of Little Big Horn. A huge granite bust of the Sioux leader sets atop the grave. The brand "Chey-Rock" was so named because it was to be distributed to both the Cheyenne River Sioux Tribe (Minnicon Jou) and the Standing Rock Sioux Tribe (Yanktonia & Hunkpapa). Chey-Rock was bottled and sold up through the 1950s, but it is vague as to when it was discontinued. The only bottle with that brand was a small 7 ounce, dated 1948, and displaying a picture of the grave site monument. The plant still exists today, property of the Coca-Cola Bottling Co., and is manned by a hand full of employees. (This info was extracted from an article entitled "The Chey-Rock Story" by S.O. Danet in the May 1991 issue of SODA NET, the official newsletter for Painted label bottle collectors).—37, 38

Chicago Club—41

Chug-a-lug—41

Churchill's—An etched drinking glass exists marked "aloha root beer"—55

Circle-A—37, 38

Circle K—Circle K Corp., Phoenix, AZ—41, 44

Clarion—Pennsylvania, c. 1952—23, 25

Claey's—Claey's Candy Inc., South Bend, IN, since 1919—116

Clear'oc—New Bedford, MA—14

Clearock—Abele Btl Works Inc., Peekskill, NY—37, 38

Cleve 'O' Club—14

Click—Click Corp of America, Conshowockin, PA. Slogan, "Drink a click (the root brew) root beer, be a winner."—41, 44, 115

Clicquot Club—Millis, Mass. c. 1881—14, 19, 37, 38, 41, 44, 86

Clipper—Clark's Beverages, Newcastle, Maine c. 1954—23, 25

Clover Club—Clover Club Beverage Co., Chicago, IL—41, 44

Cloverdale—Cloverdale Spring Co., Harrisburg, PA c. 1944—37

Club Deluxe—Bottled by Silver Springs Co., Madison, Wisconsin, distributed by Liquor Sales Co., Madison, WI.—14, 20

Club House—41

Cola—Cola Root Beer Bottling Co., Santa Ana, CA, c. 1948—23, 25

Connie's—2, 73

Consumer's—37

Convenient Food Marts—Interstate Canning Co., Louisville, KY—41, 44

Co-op—Mid-eastern Coop Inc., Carlstadt, NJ—41, 44

Cordone's—New York, c. 1949.—37, 38

Corr, Robert—R.J. Corr Naturals Inc., Chicago, Illinois c. 1985—41, 44

Cott—Cott Corp., Manchester, New Hampshire—37, 41, 44

Cotton Club—41

Country Club—41

Country's Delight—Certified Grocers Midwest Inc, Hodgkins, IL—41, 44

Country Fair—Country Fair Inc., Erie, PA—41, 44

CP—Certified Products, Minneapolis, MN—65

Cragmont—Safeway grocery store brand. Home office, Oakland, CA—37, 41, 43

Craig's—Tennessee—23

Crass—Chambersburg Coca-Cola Btl Wks, Chambersburg, PA. c. 1947—37, 38, 41

Cray's, P.J.—Holyoke, MA—11

Cre-mel—2, 73, 109

Croce—65

Crown Bottling Co.—New Kensington & Leechburg, PA—40

Crush—Orange Crush Bottlers, Quincy, IL—37, 38

Crystal—Crystal Coca-Cola Bottling Co., Tucson, AZ—23, 26, 37, 41, 44

Crystal Club—Crystal Soda Water Co., Scranton, PA—41

Cue—New York, NY—41

Custom—Custom Beverage Packers Inc., Aurora, OH—41, 44

Dad's—Dad's Root Beer Co., Chicago, IL founded in 1937. One of the major root beer companies in existence today.—2, 12—14, 17, 23, 26, 37, 38, 41, 45, 55—57, 61—63, 70, 72, 73, 87, 88, 92, 94, 95, 99, 103—106, 109—113

Daisy—Kohl Corp., Milwaukee, WI—41, 44

Dana—37

Dandy—53

Dart Drug—Dart Drug Corp., Landover, MD—41, 44

Days—37

Deborah—40

De Freesti—11

Del Monte—Del Monte Corp., San Francisco, CA—41, 45

Delta—41

Diamant—Diamant Bros Beverage Co., San Leandro, CA c. 1958—37, 38

Diamond Head—Diamond Head Beverage Inc., Honolulu, Hawaii—41, 44

Diet-Rite—Produced under authority of Royal Crown Cola, Columbus, Georgia—37, 38, 41, 44

Diett—Diett Beverage Co., College Point, NY—45

Dirigo—37

Dis-go—41

Dixi—Dixi Cola Inc., Baltimore, MD—41, 44

Dlite—Shasta Beverage Inc., Hayward, CA—41, 44

Doc's—Fajar Corp., Hammonton, NJ—41, 45

Dodger—37

Dog 'n Suds—A root beer drive-in chain started in Champagne, Illinois in 1953 by two music teachers, Jim Griggs & Don Hamacher. The original logo, a dog like character holding a mug, was picked from an art contest at the local college. The artist had drawn the picture in such a hurry, it was almost undecipherable. When it was returned to the artist for an explanation, he scribbled "dog" & "suds" with an arrow pointing to each object. The two teachers liked the idea and used it just as it was. It is unknown when the logo changed to the tap handle. At its peak in 1959-60, over 500 drive-ins existed in 38 states. As of 1988, there were less than 25 mostly located in Illinois and Indiana. Mr. Don McNutt (see info under B/K root beer) assured me that "Dog 'n Suds" was definitely a root beer in itself, but was not identified as such in the logo.—73, 74, 110

Donald Duck—General Beverages Inc., Chattanooga, TN—37, 38, 41, 45

Donner—Truckee Soda Works, Truckee, CA—14, 23

Douglas—53

Dove—Frank Tea & Spice Co., Cincinnati, OH—9

Dr. Brown's—K.B.I. College Point, NY—41, 44

Dr. Murphy's—Boston, MA—65, 67

Dr. Mutch's—37

Dr. Stearn's—Albert Lea Bottling Works, Albert Lea, MN. An ACL bottle, c. 1958 exists. Unable to substantiate if same brand listed as "Stearn's" on the pottery mugs. Will be considered as two separate brands for now.—23, 27

Dr. Swett's—Boston, MA. Famous recipe of Dr. George Washington Swett. There are claims that this brand used to produced root beer as early as 1845, prior to Hire's in 1876. Unsubstantiated. Their logos state "since 1845," but may be referring to the company rather than root beer per se.—11, 14, 22, 23, 27, 37, 38, 40, 55, 62, 64, 65, 66, 114, 118

Dub-L-Valu—97

Duchess—West Coast Grocery Co., Tacoma, WA—41, 45

Duffy's—Duffy's Inc., Denver, CO. Founded in 1929 by Frank Duffy, after being fired from managing the Colorado Coca-Cola plants during the 1920s. By 1959, with a 20 truck fleet and 8 flavors of natural fruit soft drinks including root beer, sales were nearly 3 million dollars with an estimate of 1 million cases produced annually. Duffy had coined such slogans for his advertising as "Tops in Pops," "Rainbow Flavors" and "Thirst Come—Thirst Served". Several of these slogans have been seen on other unrelated soda bottles, but the connection is unknown. Mr. Duffy himself also designed the bottle insignia and the bottle caps. In 1969, Duffy's had become the largest, private, nonfranchise soft drink company in the region. It made 22 different drinks and employed 40 people. Soon thereafter, Duffy's was bought by the Domenico's, who had formerly operated the Royal Crown Bottling Co. in Denver until 1968. (Information gathered herein was extracted from The CERVIS Journal, 22 Oct 1969, page 1 and from the Denver Post, 19 Apr 1959, page 1E). The final site for Duffy's was a 65,000 sq ft building at #111 Larimer Street, Denver, CO.—14, 16, 37, 38, 41, 62, 64, 104

Price Guide

Page	Position	Price
	title page	5-10
	T	5-15 each
	B	20-35
	C	75-100
	R	1-2 each
		35-50
	B	5-10 each
	BR	2-5 each
	BR (Pa-poose)	10-15
	BR (Puritan)	10-15
0	TL	5-10 each
	C	5-10 each
	BL	3-5 each
	BR	15-20
1	C	40-50
	CR	50-75
	B	40-50 each
2		125-150
3	TL	40-50 each
	TR	5-10 each
	B	1-3 each
4	TL (l-r)	35-40, 5-10
	TR (l-r)	15-20, 3-5, 40-50
5	L	100-125
	R	5-10 each
6	TL	15-20
	TR (Schwartz)	15-20
	TR (Vess)	5-10
	BL	5-15 each
	BR	5-10 each
7	TL	5-10 each
	BL	10-15 each
	R	75-100
8	TL	10-15 each
	CL	5-10
	CR	1-3 each
	B	10-15 each
9	TL	5-10 each
	TR	1-3 each
	B	1-2 each
0	TL	5-10
	TR	3-5
	BL	3-5 each
	BR	3-5 each
1	TL	2-3 each
	TR	2-3 each
	BL	2-3
	BR	1-2
2	TL (t-b)	1-2, 3-5, 3-5
	TR	2-3 each
	BL	1-2
	CR	3-5 each
	BR	5-10
3	TL	2-3 each
	TL (Donner)	5-10
	TR	2-3 each
4	L	4-8 each
	C (Bakers)	10-15
	C (Barrelhead)	3-5
	R	5-10 each
5	TL	30-40
	TR (l-r)	10-15, 10-15, 3-5
	BL	5-15 each
	BR	20-25 each
6	TL	10-15
	TR (l-r)	5-10, 15-20, 20-25
	BL	5-10 each
	BR	5-10 each
7	TL (Dr. Stearns)	25-35
	TL (others)	5-10 each

Page	Position	Price
	TR	3-5 each
	BL	5-10 each
	BR (Harls)	15-20
	BR (others)	5-10 each
28	TL	3-5 each
	TR	5-10 each
	BL	3-10 each
	BR	4-8 each
29	TL	5-15 each
	TR	20-25 each
	BL	30-35
	BR (l-r)	3-5, 25-35, 3-5
30	TL	10-15 each
	TR	4-8 each
	BL (32 oz)	10-15
	BL (others)	3-5
	BR	10-15
31	TL	5-10 each
	TR	30-35
	BL	40-45
	BR	3-5 each
32	TL	3-5 each
	TR	5-10 each
	BL	35-40
	BR	5-10 each
33	TL	75-100
	TR	30-40
	BL	30-40
	BR	15-20 each
34	TL	3-5 each
	TR	100-125 each
	BL	4-8 each
	BR	50-60
35	TL	5-10 each
	CR	5-10 each
	BL	5-10 each
36	TL (Uncle Bens)	20-25
	TL (Victory)	15-20
	TR (l-r)	50-75, 75-100
	BL	10-15 each
	BR (l-r)	3-5, 20-25, 10-15
38	BL	3-5 each
	BR	3-5 each
39	TL	3-5 each
	TR	3-5 each
	BL	3-5 each
	BR	3-5 each
40	CL (Deborah)	10-15
	CL (others)	3-5 each
	CR	10-15 each
	BL	15-20 each
43	TL	5-10 each
	TR	5-10 each
	CL	5-10 each
	BL (Bestyet)	10-15
	BL (Bells)	15-20
	BL (others)	5-10 each
	BR	15-20
44	TL (flat top)	3-5
	TL (cone tops)	10-20 each
	TR	10-20 each
	CL	3-5 each
	CR (Camelot)	10-15
	CR (others)	5-10 each
	BL	5-10 each
	BR (Daisy)	15-20
	BR (others)	5-10 each
45	TL	15-20 each
	CL (left end)	25-35
	CL (others)	3-10 each
	CR	50-75

Page	Position	Price
	BL	5-10 each
	BR	5-10 each
46	TL	5-10 each
	TR	5-10 each
	CL	5-10 each
	BL	3-10 each
	BR	5-10 each
47	TL	5-10 each
	TR (Holiday Inn)	20-25
	TR (others)	10-15 each
	C	5-10 each
	B	5-10 each
48	TL (Klondike)	15-20
	TL (King Kooler)	15-20
	TL (others)	5-10 each
	TR	5-10 each
	CL (Lawsons)	15-20
	CL (others)	5-10 each
	CR	20-25 each
	BL	20-30 each
	BR	20-30 each
49	TL (Mr Root Beer)	15-20
	TL (others)	5-10 each
	TR (Pabst)	25-35
	TR (others)	5-10 each
	CL	5-10 each
	CR	5-10 each
	B	5-10 each
50	TL	5-10 each
	TR	5-10 each
	CL (Root 66)	10-15 each
	CL (others)	5-10 each
	CR	5-10 each
	BR	5-10 each
51	T	10-15 each
	CL	5-10 each
	CR (Tico)	20-25
	CR (Two Guys)	25 -30
	CR (others)	5-10 each
	BL	5-10 each
	BR (Uncle Jakes)	15-20
	BR (others)	5 -10 each
52	T	5-10 each
	C (Yukon)	10-15
	C (Yukon Club)	10-15
	C (others)	5-10 each
	B	1-3 each
53	BL	500-800
	BR	500-800
54	TL	300-500
	TR	15-25
	BL	200-400
	BR (reproduction)	15-25
	BR (original)	300-500
55	TR (l-r)	20-30, 3-5, 20-30
	B	20-30 each
56	TL (l-r)	5-10, 10-15
	TR	5-10 each
	BL	5-10 each
	BR	15-20
57	R	10-15
	L	25-30
58	TL	5-10
	TR	5-10
	BL	5-10
	BR	25-35
59	TL	5-10
	R	5-10
	BL	3-5
60	TL	2-3
	TR	2-3
	BL	2-3

Page	Position	Price
	BR	3-5
61	TL	2-3
	TR	1-2
	BL	2-3
	BR	1-2
62	B	5-10 each
63	TL	3-5 each
	TR	5-10 each
	B	3-5 each
64	T .	3-5 each
	C	2-3 each
	B (Hires)	1-3
	B (A&W di-cuts)	10-15 each
65	B	200-250
66	TL	100-125
	TR	40-60 each
	CL	100-125
	CR	200-250
	BL (Goose)	50-75
	BL (A&W)	20-25
67	TL (l-r)	35-50, 35-50, 20-25
	CL (l-r)	40-60, 30-40, 40-60
	CR	100-125
	BL (l-r)	60-75, 35-45
	BR	40-60 each
68	T (l-r)	40-60, 60-75, 50-75
	C	35-50 each
	B	35-50 each
69	T (l-r)	50-75, 150-200
	B	40-60 each
70	C	30-40 each
	B	35-45 each
71	TL	35-45 each
	CL	20-30 each
	R	1-3
	BL (Frostie)	5-10
	BL (others)	35-45 each
72	TL	35-45 each
	TR	30-40 each
	CL	45-60 each
	CR (Triple XXX)	45-60
	CR (others)	30-40
	BL	35-45 each
	BR	20-30
73	T	3-10 each
	C (l-r)	15-20, 20-25, 10-15, 10-15
	B	10-20 each
74	T (dog logo)	10-15 each
	T (sign logo)	5-10 each
	C	10-20 each
	B (Menlo)	15-25
	B (others)	5-10 each
75	T	15-20 each
	C	15-20 each
	B	15-20 each
76	T (O-So)	10-15
	T (Jocko's)	20-25
	CR	10-20 each
	CL (Nesbitt's)	20-25
	CL (others)	10-15 each
	B (Mugs-up)	10-15 each
	B (Little Skip)	25-35 each
77	T	40-50 each
	C (TNT)	25-30
	C (Park Lane)	25-30
	C (others)	5-10 each
	B	5-10 each
78	T	15-25 each
	C	15-25 each
	B	3-5 each
79	L	15-25
	R	5-10
80	TL	10-15 each
	C (Hires)	10-15
	C (others)	15-20 each
	B	15-20
81	TL	20-25
	BL	20 -25
	R	10-15
82	TL (l-r)	15-20, 25-30
	C (l-r)	10-15, 15-20, 10-15
	B (l-r)	15-20, 20-25, 5-10
83	T	5-10 each
	B	15-20
84	T	5-10 each
	CL	20-25
	C	10-15
	CR	10-15
	BL	15-20
	BR	20-25
85	T (girl)	25-30
	T (hand)	50-60
	C	10-15
	B	10-15
86	L	200-250
	R	45-55
87	T	40-45
	R	45-50
	B (l-r)	30-35, 15-20
88	TL	50-60
	TR	5-10
	BL	3-5
	BR	20-25
89	TL	60-75
	TR	25-30
	CR	75-100
	BL	60-75
	BR	60-75
90	T	45-55
	CR	35-50
	CL	40-50
	B	60-75
91	T	30-35
	CR	50-60
	L	125-150
	BR	1000-1200
92	T	45-55
	CR	65-75
	L	75-100
	BR	75-85
93	TL	60-75
	TR	15-20
	B	45-55
94	TL	65-75
	CR	65-75
	BL	65-75
	BR	65-75
95	TL	150-200
	TR	45-55
	BL	125-150
	BR	75-85
96	TL	15-20
	TR (Golden Bridge)	45-55
	TR (Richardson)	20-25
	BL	125-150
	BR	10-15
97	TL	35-45
	TR	300-400
	BL	20-30
	BR	65-75
98	L	45-55
	C	55-65
	R	25-35
99	TL	45-55
	TR	100-125
	BL	25-35
	BR	65-80
100	TL	65-75
	L	10-15
	R	35-45
	BR	125-150
101	TR	10-15
	BL	20-25
	BR	55-65
102	T	100-125
	CL	5-10
	CR	25-35
	BR (l-r)	10-15, 5-10
103	TL	35-40
	TR (l-r)	1-3, 5-10
	BL	35-45
	BR (large bear)	35-45
	BR (small bear)	10-1 5
104	TL	20-25
	TR (case only)	50-60
	BL (t-b)	45-55, 15-20, 45-55
	BR	200-250
105	TL	5-10
	TR (l-r)	30-40, 10-15, 35-45, 3-5
	BL	15-20
	BR	5-10 each
106	TL (l-r)	10-15, 5-10, 10-15
	TR	10-15
	CL	3-5 each
	BL (t-b)	15-20, 20-25
107	T	35-45
	BL	45-55
	R	3-5
108	TL	3-5
	TR	15-20 each
	BL	3-5
	CR	10-15 each
	BR	3-5 each
109	T	3-5 each
	CR (Hires boy)	25-35
	CR (Mr root beer)	25-35
	CR (others)	5-10 each
	B (Rochester)	20-25
	B (others)	5-10 each
110	TL	15-25 each
	TR	150-200
	CL	20-30 each
	CR	65-80
	BL	10-15 each
111	TL	1-3
	TR	5-10 each
	CL	5-10
	CR	50-75
	BL (t-b)	5-10, 3-5
112	TL	3-5
	CL (marbles only)	20-25
	CR	15-25 each
	BL	15-20
	BR	15-20
113	TL (l-r)	5-10, 1-2, 10-15
	TR	10-15
	CL	75-100
114	TL	10-15
	TR (l-r)	1-2, 5-10
	CR	20-25
	BL	5-10 each
	BR	20-25
115	TL (American)	25-30
	TL (Hires)	10-15
	TR	5-10 each
	BL	20-25
	BR (l-r)	15-20, 5-10, 1-3
116	TL	all 3-5
	CL	all 5-10
	CR (l-r)	10-15, 5-10
	BL	1-2
	BR	5-10
117	TL	5-10
	TC	5-10
	TR	20-25
	BL	15-20
	BC	1-2
	CR	2-3
118	L	45-55
	T	15-25
	CR	75-100
	BR	600-800

Not doing much business in its later years, the doors were finally closed in 1988. **THE LEGEND OF MANITOU**—Indians of the Colorado Rocky Mountains discovered the magical spring hidden in a secret valley in the shadow of Pikes Peak. The Indians believed that the Great Spirit "Manitou" (The Peaceful One), lived deep within the spring, and his breath made the cool clear water bubble and sparkle.—14, 17

Dark" did MUG television commercials for several years. Today, Mug is owned by Pepsico.—14, 24, 32, 38, 39, 42, 49, 55, 56, 78, 116

Mugs-Up—By the looks of the logo, it was probably a drive-in style restaurant of the 1950s. The logo was a mug with its contents pouring out and down onto a small building. No other information is available.—73, 76

Murray's—53

My Pop's—My Pop's Root Beer Co., Philadelphia, PA—24, 32, 38, 39, 42

Myopia Club—Myopia Club Beverage Co., Islington, MA—38, 39

Nancy Jane—Dist by Southwest Wholesale, Packed by Pacific Filling, Haward, CA.—42, 49

Napa Rock—Napa Rock Mineral Water Co., Oakland, CA—14, 22

Natco—38

National—A can indicates National Tea Co., Chicago, IL., c. 1976. A crown indicates National Bottling Co., Saginaw, MI.—38, 39, 42, 49

Nehi—Originally known as Chero-Cola, Royal Crown created the Nehi brand in 1924. In 1934, the Nehi Corporation introduced Royal Crown Cola. Now a product of the Royal Crown Cola Co., Columbus, GA.—38, 39, 42, 48, 92

Nesbitt's—Nesbitt's, Doraville, GA. During the 1944 St. Louis beverage convention, a bottler named Nesbitt, owner of Nesbitt's Orange in California, was hit over the head with a beer bottle and killed. (Soda Net article "The St. Louis Soda Wars" taken from The South County Journal, 7/20/88, -Soda Net, Nov 1990 issue)—38, 39, 42, 49, 73, 76

Newport Club—42, 49

New York Seltzer—New York Seltzer, Walnut, CA c. 1986—14, 19

Niagara—38, 39

Nine-O-Five—9-0-5 Stores, St Louis, MO—42. 49

No Cal—Kirsch Beverage Co., Brooklyn, NY c. 1952. Considered the first low calorie soft drink.—15, 23, 42

Nodak—38, 39

Norka—Norka Beverage Co., Akron, OH. Norka Beverage Co. was founded by Jacob Paquin, an immigrant from France, in 1924. Throughout its existence, the 14 flavors produced remained at a limited distribution within the general area of Akron. In 1962, the family business was liquidated. The brand name was taken from the name of the town spelled backwards.—90

Norwest—42

Nutro—38, 39

Nyman's—Nyman's Extract Co., Chicago, IL—9, 10

Ol' Smoothie—Ol' Smoothie Co., Pine City, MN—24, 32, 42, 49

Old Castle Co.—38

Old Colonial—Colonial Bottling Works, Pittsburg & Philadelphia—11

Old Colony—38, 39, 42

Old Dutch—Dist by Fitz's Beverage Inc., Maryland Heights, MO—42, 49, 62

Old Fashioned—Health Valley, Montebello, CA—15, 19

Old Frontier—100

Old Jug—James Esposito Co., Philadelphia, PA—38, 39

Old Kentucky—65, 67

Old Newbury—C. Leary & Co., Newbury Port, MA. (Leary also had a root beer)—38, 39

Old San Francisco Seltzer—Old San Francisco Seltzer, South El Monte, CA. 1986—15, 19

Old Time—Roundy's Inc., Milwaukee, WI. As of 1988, the product was available in 2 liter bottles only.—15, 21, 24, 42, 49

Olliver's—38

O'neal's—38

Oneta Club—Ohio—38

On-Tap—Pepsico Inc., Purchase, NY—24, 38, 42, 49, 73, 77

Ontario—42

Orchard Park—Orchard Park Foods Inc, Buffalo, NY—42, 49

O-So—Bottled by Canada Dry of Muskegon Inc., Muskegon, MI. Slogan: "O-So-Good"—15, 19, 38, 39, 73, 76

Our Family—Nash Finch Co., Minneapolis, MN—42, 49

Ozark Maid—38

Pabst—Pabst Brewing Co., Milwaukee, WI—42, 49

Pacemaker—42

Pantry Pride—Pantry Products Inc., (division of Food Fair Inc.), Philadelphia, PA.—42, 49

Papoose—E.A. Zatarain & Sons, New Orleans, LA c. 1889—9, 24, 40, 65

Pappy's—Eagle Soft Drink Co., S. Milwaukee, WI—38

Parade—National Brand Sales, Parkridge, IL—38, 42, 49

Park—Jewel Companies, Inc., Barrington, IL—42, 49

Park Club—42

Park Lane—73, 77

Parson's—Natural Soda Sales Co., Atlanta, GA—42, 49

Par-T-Pak—38, 39, 42

Party Club—Commander Foods Inc., Syracuse, NY—42, 49

Pathmark—Supermarkets General Corp, Woodbridge, NJ c. 1987—42, 49

Patio—Pepsi-Cola Co., Purchase, NY—38, 39, 42, 49

Peacock—Peacock Beverage Co., Chicago, IL

Peer—42

Peerless—15

Penguin—Grand Union Co., Elmwood Park, NJ—42

Peoples—Peoples Drug Stores Inc., Alexandria, VA—42

Pep-Ade—Pep-Ade Flavor Products, Chicago, IL—105

Pequot—Pequot Spring Water Co., Glastonbury, CT c. 1969—38, 39

Peter's—Try Me Bottling Co., Birmingham, AL—24

Pic-Nic—38

Piggly Wiggly—Piggly Wiggly Corp., Jacksonville, FL—42, 48

Pik-A-Pop—Pik-A-Pop Inc., Pasco, WA—38, 39

Pilsen-Pilsen Products Co., Chicago, IL. Slogan: "Best by Test."—96

Pin-Mar—42

Pioneer—Pioneer Soda Bottling Works, Davenport, WA. A small family business established by the Einbeck's about 1900. Because of no outside hired help, when the last family member was incapable of continuing production, the doors were finally closed in 1982. The small plant, attached to the original house they started in, remained intact and all equipment, supplies and stock were left untouched. (An in depth article can be found in SODA NET, March 1991, entitled "Opening a Time Capsule of the Soda Bottling Industry," submitted by Ron Fowler of Seattle, WA. It is a reprint from the October 1985 issue of Old Bottle Magazine).—15, 22

Pioneer—Pioneer Food Stores Cooperative, Inc., Carlstadt, NJ. (There is no evidence of.any connection between this brand and the preceding Pioneer brand. The can representing this brand is date-stamped 1982)—42, 49

Pix—Publix Supermarkets Inc., Hq Lakeland, FL—42, 49

Plaza—H.E.B. Food Stores, Corpus Christi, TX c. 1974—42, 49

Plus—Plus Discount Food Inc., Montvale, NJ—42, 49

Pocono—Avion Management Corp, Rochester, NY—42, 49

Polar—Polar Corp., Worcester, Mass—42, 49

Polar Bear—9

Polly's—Independence Bottling Co., Independence, MO. c. 1947. Founded by Polly Compton. The plant closed about 1967 and the building was demolished and the site became a park—Polly's Park. It is reported that each parrot on the bottle was colored to correspond to the flavor contents.—89

Pop—Braser Pop Kola Co., Atlanta, GA—38, 39

Pop-O—United Grocers Ltd, Richmond, CA. c. 1968.—42, 44

Pop-Over—Milton, FL—12

Pop Shoppe—Pop Shoppes of America, Denver, CO—38, 39

Portage—Portage Root Beer Co., Portage, WI—12

Price Chopper—Price Chopper Inc., Schenectady, NY—42, 49

Pri-Pak—42

Provigo—42

Publix—Publix Supermarkets Inc., Hq Lakeland, FL—42

Purdy—Purdy Root Beer Co., Portage, WI—12

Puritan—Keller Products Co., Chicago, IL—9

Purity—38

Purity Supreme—Purity Supreme, Inc., Billerica, MA c. 1977—42, 49

QT—Quicktrip Corp., Tulsa, OK—42, 49

Quaker—Ratay Bottling Co., East St. Louis, IL c. 1962.—24

Queen-O—New York c. 1960s—38, 39

Queen of Scot—Scot Lad Foods, Inc., Lansing, IL—42, 49

Quevic—(See Saratoga)

R—7 Up Bottling Co., Cedar City, UT—38, 39

Rain-bo—Salida, CO.—38, 39

Rainbow—Aluminum can indicates Fleming Co. Inc., Oklahoma City, OK. Earlier pieces indicate brand began c. 1938.—38, 42, 49, 73, 77

Ralph's—Ralph's Grocery Co., Los Angeles, CA—42, 49

Ramages—Ramage's Beverages, Salem, OR c. 1954—38, 39

Ramblin'—Product of the Coca-Cola Company. This brand is served at Denny's Restaurants and is listed on the menu.—24, 32, 38, 42, 49, 73, 77, 111

Rand's—38

Raser's—John B. Raser, Manufacturing Druggist, Reading, PA—9, 79, 80

Red & White—Red & White Int'l, (Federated Foods), Park Ridge, IL—42, 49

Red Arrow—Red Arrow Bottling Co., Detroit, MI—38, 39

Red Owl—Red Owl Marketing Corp., Minneapolis, MN—42, 49

Red Robe—General Grocer Co., St Louis, MO—15, 16

Red Rock Bottling Co.—Westfield, WI—15, 20

Reed's—113

Reed & Bell—62, 73, 77

Regent—Pittsburgh, PA—38, 42

Rex—Bottle indicates Louisiana Coca-Cola Bottling Co., New Orleans, LA. Can indicates Refreshment Ent., Gretna, LA.—24, 32, 42, 50

Richardson's—Richardson's Corp., Rochester, NY. Some items show "Richardson's Liberty root beer" which may have resulted from a merger or buy-out since Liberty was an older, smaller company.—24, 32, 38, 39, 57, 60, 65, 70, 73, 77, 88, 93, 96, 97, 115

Richfood—Richfood Inc., Richmond, VA—42

Ritz—The can says packed by Beverage Canners, Miami, FL—38, 42, 50

Riverside—42

Rob's—Charles C. Copeland Co., Milton & Brockton, MA—24

Rochester—J. Hungerford Smith Co., Rochester, NY—53, 55, 70, 72, 86, 95, 109, 110, 114

Rock Spring—38

Rocky Top—Bluefield Beverage Co., Bluefield, VA—42, 49

Rondo—38

Root 66—Anheuser Busch, St. Louis, MO. Produced by their soft drink division in 1979 as a limited edition. Possibly in honor of Route 66—an East-West bound national highway from Chicago to Los Angeles through the Southwestern part of the United States. Now known as Highway 40. A popular old song exists called "Route 66." A popular TV program of the same name aired during the 1950s.—42, 50

Rooti—A product of the Canada Dry Corporation. A series with the bear in various poses.—42, 50

Rosebud—Texas—12, 13, 24, 33

Royal—38

Royal Crown—Began by Claude A. Hatcher, a grocer, in 1905 in Columbus, Georgia with the bottling of a ginger ale and a root beer. Created the Nehi brand (formally known as Chero-Cola) in 1924. The Nehi Corp., in turn, introduced Royal Crown Cola in 1934.—12

Royal Family—38, 39

Royal Flush—38

Royal Islands—42

Royal Palm—42, 50

Royal Worchester—9

Ruby—A fountain syrup dispenser exists.—53

Ryan—103

SA—SuperAmerica, St. Paul Park, MN—42, 50

S&H—(see Simmons & Hammond)

S&S—70, 72

Salute—Dr. Pepper Co., Dallas, TX—42, 50

San Francisco—(See Old San Francisco)

Sanders—38

Santa Fe Trail—Denver—38, 39

Saratoga—New York—40

Sarsaparilla—Health Valley, Montebello, CA—15, 19

Sav-On—Sav-on Drug Stores Inc., Marina Del Rey, CA—42, 50

Schilling—McCormick & Co. Inc., Hunt Valley, MD. Produces a line of baking & spice products found on grocery shelves today.—9

Schmidt's—38

Schnuck's—Schnuck Markets Inc., Bridgeton, MO—42, 50

Schueler—Schueler Brothers Inc., Stamford, CT—24, 33

Schuster—Schuster Co., Cleveland, OH—65, 67, 118

Schuylkill—38

Schwartz—Schwartz Ginger Ale Co., San Francisco, CA—15, 16

Schweppe's—42

Scot Lad—Scot Lad Food Inc., Chicago, IL—42, 50

Scotch Buy—Safeway Stores, Oakland, CA—42, 50

Scotty—Associated Grocer's Co., St Louis, MO—42, 50

Scramble—Canner's of Eastern Arkansas, West Memphis, Ark.—42, 50

Sentry—42

7-11—Seven-Eleven Convenient Stores, Southland Corp, Dallas, TX—42, 50

'76—American '76 Co., Palatine, IL—42, 50

Seymour—Seymour Beverages Co., Seymour, WI—15, 23

Shank's—9

Shasta—Shasta Beverage Inc., Hayward, CA—42, 50, 55, 56, 113

Shop 'n Bag—Shop'n Bag Marketing, Philadelphia, PA—42, 50

Shopper's Value—Preferred Products Inc., Eden Prairie, MN—42, 50

Shop Rite—Wakefern Food Corp., Elizabeth, NJ c. 1976—42, 50

Shopwell—Distributed by Daitch Crystal Dairies, Inc., New York, NY—42, 50

Shortstop—Shortstop Stores, Concord, CA—42, 50

Shrader & Johnson—(see Mexican)

Shurfine—Shurfine-Central Corp., Northlake, IL—42, 50

Silverfross—73, 78

Silver Spring—Walpole Bottling Co., Walpole, MA—42, 50

Simmons, A.D.—(see A.D. Simmons)

Simmons & Hammond—Portland, Maine—110

Simpson Springs—Simpson Spring Co., S. Easton, MA c. 1979—42, 50

Singer's—15

Skagg's—American Stores Buying Co., Salt Lake City, UT—42, 50

Skyhigh—Diamond Bottling Works, Milwaukee, WI. "Old style draft root beer like mother made."—24, 33, 104

Slender—Beverage Marketing Inc., St. Paul, MN c. 1977—42, 50

Smash—Kohl Corp., Milwaukee, WI—42, 50

Smile—Mahaska Bottling Co., Oskaloosa, IA—42, 50

Smithsonian—Rochester, NY. A sign exists.

Smitty's—Michigan—24

Snaider's—

Snow Peak—American Beverage Corp., College Point, NY—42, 50

Snowy Peak—Safeway Stores, Oakland, CA—38, 39, 42, 50

Soda Barrel—Soda Barrel Co., Camden, NJ—15

Soda Hut—42

Soda King—Packed by 7-Up Bottling Co., San Francisco, CA—42, 50

Soho—Started in Sophia's kitchen in 1977, by Sophia Collier & Connie Best, in Brooklyn, NY. Named after New York's famous artist neighborhood. Canned under auth of the American Natural Beverage Co., NY, NY—15, 18, 42, 50

Solon Springs—Ohio—38

Sonny O'Gold—Illinois c 1948—24

Sparco—Sparkling Spring Water Co., Kenosha, WI. Closed in 1982—15, 20

Sparkeeta—Sparkletts Drinking Water Corp.. Los Angeles, CA—24, 33, 38, 62, 63

Sparkel—Purity Stores Inc., Burlingame, CA—38, 42, 50

Sparkletts—Sparkletts Drinking Water Corp, Los Angeles, CA—15, 18

Sparkling—Pennsylvania c. 1948—24

Spartan—42

Sprecher's—Currently being produced. Milwaukee, WI—38, 39

Spree—Shasta Beverage Co., Hayward, CA—42, 50

Springfield—Certified Grocers of California, Los Angeles, CA—42, 50

Spurgeon's—Centralia, Washington—38

Squeeze—38, 39, 42

Staff—Staff Supermarket Assoc., Jericho, NY—42, 50

Standard—Standard Bottling Co., Denver, CO. Founded in 1886 by Fred Durocher Sr. The plant was located at the corner of 13th and Lawrence, Denver, CO. The phone numbers were Main 65 and Main 66. The company produced filtered artesian water, various brands of ginger ale, root beer, soda, beer, fountain fruits and syrups. It had a fleet of 20 trucks and cars, employed 30-50 people, and distributed its products throughout Colorado and the surrounding states. A unique feature was an 800 foot deep artesian well, drilled about 1914 and lined with glazed concrete. It was free from contaminating bacteria and germs and thus provided a source of pure soft water to be used in all Standard's beverages. The plant was sold to the Canada Dry Co. in 1948. Fred Durocher died in 1954. In 1953, Canada Dry vacated the building, and in 1954, the 3 story, 125 feet square building was torn down to make room for an expanding Carlson-Frink Co. plant. (Source for information was "The Colorado Manufacturer and Consumer," June 1931, Vol 16, No. 12 and "The Denver Post" Mar 4, 1954, page 33.)—15, 18, 38, 39, 118

Star Bottling Works—Philadelphia, PA—38, 39

Star Ice & Soda—Star Ice & Soda Works, Wailuku, Maui, HI—38

Stars—Star Market Co., (Div of Jewel Co.,) Cambridge, MA—42, 50

Stater Bros.—Stater Bros. Markets, Colton, CA—42, 50

Stayung—42

Steinberger's—38, 39

Stearn's—Unable to substantiate if same brand listed as "Dr. Stearn's" on the ACL bottles of c. 1958. They will be considered as separate for now.—53, 65, 67

Steven's—Steven's 7-Up Bottling Co., McCook, NE c. 1947—38, 39

Stewart's—Started as a root beer stand in Springfield, OH in 1924 by Frank Stewart. Sold root beer and popcorn. First drive-in began in Mansfield, OH in 1925. Franchising commenced in 1931. At its peak, 170 drive-ins existed. As of 1989, 68 existed mainly in New Jersey and West Virginia with a few scattered throughout the Northeastern area. Home office is Stewart's Restaurants, Inc., 114 W. Atlantic Ave., Clementon, NJ.—15, 24, 34, 70, 72, 73, 78, 111

Stites—Stites Root Beer Co., Sioux Falls, SD.—65, 66

Stone Jug—38, 39

Stop & Shop—Stop & Shop Supermarkets, Boston, MA—38, 42, 50

Stop-n-Go—Packed for Stop-n-Go Foods, Inc., Trotwood, OH—42

Stratford—24

Strickler's—9

Suburban—Allegheny Pepsi-Cola Bottling Co., Baltimore, MD c. 1974—42, 50

Sunbow—38, 39

Sunburst—38, 39

Suncrest—38, 39

Sunday Funnies—Flavor Valley Corp., NY, NY. Consists of a set of 4 cans, each with a different character on the front: Beetle Bailey, Blondie, Popeye, and Hagar the Horrible. Each can's reverse features a comic strip of the character. (Note: There are 7 different comic strips for each character, providing a grand total of 28 cans for the series.)—42, 51

Sun-Glo—Brooks Products Inc., Holland, MI—42, 50

Sun Glory—Stop & Shop Supermarkets, Boston, MA—42, 51

Sunny—L.A. Beverage Co., Los Angeles, CA—38, 39

Sunny Jim—Pacific Food Products Co., Seattle, WA—42, 51

Sunnyside—Oklahoma Canning Co., Oklahoma City, OK—42, 51

Sunrise—Sunrise Inc., Marshall, MN—38, 39, 42, 51

Sunshine—Sunshine Food Stores Inc., Burton, MI c. 1979—42, 51

Sunspot—38

Super S—SSI Co., Oakland, CA—42, 51

Supreme—Supreme Drug Products, Rochester, NY—9

Sussex—42

Swallo—Kantor Bottling Co., Beloit, WI & Rockford, IL

Swallow's—G.M. Swallow's & Sons, Lima, OH—15, 20, 24, 34, 38, 39, 40, 103

Sweet Life—Sweet Life Products Co., Suffield, CT—42, 51

Sweet 'n Low—M.B.C. Beverage Inc., New York, NY—15, 42, 51

Sweet Sixteen—St. Louis, MO—38, 39

Sweet Valley—Aldi-Inc., Batavia, IL—42, 51

Swifty—42

TAB—A product of the Coca-Cola Co.—42, 51

Target—42

Tartan—42

Taste Well—42

Taylor—Prepared only by W. Scott Taylor, Chemist, Trenton, NJ c. 1890.—9, 79, 80

Taylor Maid—Taylor Beverage Inc., Hazelwood, MO—42, 51

Ted's—Moxie Co., Needham Heights-Boston, Mass. Represents Ted Williams, the baseball player. A small sign and a bottle has been reproduced featuring Ted with a bat on his shoulder.—24, 34, 38, 39, 108

Teddy's—15, 38

Ten-Erbs—Ten-Erbs Root Beer Co., Bryan Btl Wks, Bryan, OH—24

Texas—Texas Beverage Packers Inc., San Antonio, TX—42, 51

Thayer's—

Thomson & Taylor's—9, 10

Thorofare—Domont Beverage Inc., Sunman, IN—42, 51

Three Star—9

Thrifty—Thrifty Drug & Discount Stores, Los Angeles, CA—42, 51

Ticket—Custom Packaging Corp., Maryland Heights, MO—42, 51

Tico—Packed by Metro Beverage Co., Columbus, OH—42, 51

Tiger—38

Ting—Wisconsin Bottling Service, Waupaca, WI. Large company at one time, now produces only in summer. May or may not open in 1989.—15, 22, 42, 51

Tiny Tim—Tiny Tim Beverage Co., Pittsburgh, PA—38, 39

Tip Top—42

TNT—73, 77

Tolls—L.A. Beverage Co., Los Angeles, CA—38, 39

Tom Moore—Coca-Cola Bottling Midwest Inc., St Paul, MN c. 1974—38, 39, 42, 51

Tom Sawyer—Middleton Spring Beverage Co., Inc., Middleton, MA c. 1952-1963—24, 34

Tom Thumb—Tom Thumb Food Markets, Hastings, MN—42, 51

Tom Tucker—38

Topmost—General Grocer Co., St Louis, MO—42, 51

Top Treat—National Tea Co., Chicago, IL—38, 39, 42, 51

Topp—Tasty Mates Co., Camden, NJ—15, 19, 42, 51

Tops in Pops—Distributed by Von's Grocery Co., Los Angeles, CA—42, 51

Tower—Prospect Hill Bottling Co., Somerville & Charleston, MA—24, 34, 42, 63, 89, 112

Towle—Towle Mfg Co., St Paul, MN. Founded by Patrick Towle in 1888. Main product was maple syrup. A log cabin design was his logo and several containers in the shape of a log cabin were produced. The root beer extract bottle is embossed "Towle's Log Cabin Root Beer." In 1928, Towle's was purchased by the General Foods Corp.—9

Town House—38

Towne Club—Towne Club Beverage Corp., Warren, MI—38, 39

Triangle Club—Manufactured only by Montgomery Ward & Co.—9

Triple—Frank's Beverages, Philadelphia, PA—42, 51

Triple AAA—Triple AAA Co., Oklahoma City, OK.—24, 35, 38, 39, 42, 55, 56, 91, 94, 96, 106, 110

Triple XXX—Triple XXX Corp., Houston, TX. Slogan: "Makes Thirst a Joy."—24, 35, 38, 39, 42, 51, 65, 67, 70, 72, 73, 78, 102, 106

Try Me—Try Me Bottling Co., Hagerstown, MD—38, 39

Tubz—Moran Group Inc., St. Louis, MO—42, 51

TV—(True Value). Fleming Co. Inc., Topeka, KS—42, 51

Twang—Early ACL bottles dated 1948 state "bottled under auth of C.O. & W.D. Sethness Co., Chicago, IL." Later bottles dated 1956 state "bottled under auth of Twang Root Beer Co., Chicago, IL." Advertised as vitamin root beer, promotional slogan suggests "Save cap for valuable premiums."—24, 35, 38, 39, 42, 89

Twin Kiss—73, 76

Two Guys—Vornado Inc., Garfield, NJ—42, 51

UIC—Coca-Cola Bottling Co., Lamar, CO—38, 39

Uncle Ben's—Uncle Ben's Beverage Co., Wilmington, DE—24, 36

Uncle Dan's—Cadillac Ginger Ale Co., Detroit, MI., authorized by Uncle Dan's Co., Detroit, MI—15, 18, 94

Uncle Jake's—Mccoy Inc., St Paul, MN c. 1966—42, 51

Uncle Joe's—Pennsylvania—24

Uncle Smilie's—Duluth, MN—15

Uncle Tom's—San Bernadino, CA.—24

United States—United States Root Beer Co., Pittsburgh, PA—9

Unity—Kingston Marketing Co., Skokie, IL—42, 51

U-Zo—Dist by 7-Up Bottling Co., St Louis, MO—38, 39

Valley—El Dorado Brewery, Stockton, CA c. 1918—15

Valu-Check'd—Federated Foods Inc., Arlington Heights, IL—42, 52

Valu Time—Valu Time Division of Topco Assoc Inc., Skokie, IL—42, 52

Valu Vend—Valu Vend Inc., Baltimore, MD—42, 52

Variety Club—42

Varsity—Graf's Beverage Co., Milwaukee, WI—42, 51

Vegas Vic—Nevada—38, 39

Veri—White Hen Pantry (Div of Jewel Co.), Elmhurst, IL—42, 52

Vess—Vess Beverage Co., St Louis, MO—15, 16, 38, 39, 42, 52

Victory—Geo. W. Peverley Co., Pacoima, CA c. 1944—24, 36

Virginia Dare—Crown states "under franchise Virginia Dare Extract Co." Note: Virginia Dare was the 1st child born to colonial parents in America.—38, 39

Vogal's—38

Von's—Von's Grocery Co., Los Angeles, CA—42, 52

Vreeland's Indian—11

Wagner's—Tiffin, OH—11, 38

Waist Watcher's—British American Beverage Ltd, Scotia, NY—42, 52

Waldbaum's—Waldbaum Inc., Central Islip, NY—42, 52

Walker's—Quart size bottle dated 1948 states "Walker's Beverages, Plaistow, NH." Later bottles dated 1959 state "Middlesex Fells Springs, Melrose, MA."—24, 36

Walsh's—T.E. Walsh, chemist, Albany, NY—79

Walt's—Walt's Pop Dock, Springfield, MO c. 1950s—38, 39

Ward's—9

Warwick's—9

Watkin's—9

Wawa—Wawa Food Markets, Wawa, Pennsylvania—42

Weber's—Weber's Superior Root Beer Inc., Tulsa, OK c. 1933. No response to inquiries in 1989. May be closed!—15, 22, 70, 72, 73, 76

Week's—9

Wegman's—Wegman's Food Markets Inc., Rochester, NY c. 1981—42, 52

Weight Watchers—Camargo Food Inc., Cincinnati, OH c. 1976—42, 52

Weingarten—Canned exclusively for Grand Union Co., Elmwood Park, NJ. Dist by Beverage Packaging Inc., Fort Worth, TX—42, 52

Weis—Packed by Concord Beverage Co., Concordville, PA—42

Welch's—Welch Food Inc., Westfield, NY—38, 39, 42, 52

Werbelow's—Werbelow Beverage Co., Shawano, WI—15, 23

West Coast—38

Western Bottling Works—3136 Army St., San Francisco, CA—15, 21

Western Family—Western Family Foods, San Francisco, CA—42, 52

Western Valley—Associated Grocers, Phoenix, AZ—42, 52

Whistle—Stempien Beverage Co., Detroit, MI—38, 39

White Rock—White Rock Corp., Brooklyn, NY—38, 39, 42, 52

White Rose—Packed by Concord Beverage Co., Concordville, PA—38, 42, 52

Wildwood—Wildwood Sales Co., Chicago, IL c. 1975—42, 52

William's—Williams & Carleton Co., Hartford, CT c. 1896—9, 79, 82

Wilson's—Coca-Cola Bottling Co., TX c. 1953—38

Windham—38, 39

Windsor—Windsor Water & Bottling Works, Denver, CO—38

Wins—Wins Beverages Inc., Milwaukee, WI—15, 21, 38, 39

Winter Brook Seltzer—Winterbrook Corp., Seattle, WA c. 1986—15, 19

Wold's—Lemont, IL c. 1960—38

Wolverine—Wolverine Ginger Ale Co., Detroit, MI—38, 39

Woosies—Texas c. 1938—38, 39

Worley's—Worley's Beverages Inc., Selma, NC—12, 14, 24, 36

Wright—Wright Root Beer Bottling Co., Baton Rouge, LA—12, 14, 24, 36, 62

X—Pence Bros Pharmaceutical Co., Brookville, OH—38, 39

Yankee Doodle—Yankee Doodle Root Beer Co., Los Angeles, CA—15, 24, 36, 38, 39

YD—Empire Bottling Co., Malden, MA—24, 38, 39

Yosemite—San Francisco, California—38

Yukon—A&P, Montvale, NJ—42, 52

Yukon Club—A&P Tea Co., New York, NY—15, 18, 38, 39, 42, 52

Yummy—Manufactured by Itasca Processing Co. Inc., Itasca, IL. Dist by Jewel Companies Inc., Melrose Park, IL.—42, 52

Zarembo—Alaska—65

Zatarain's—E.A. Zatarain & Sons, New Orleans, LA c. 1889. (Also produced "Papoose" root beer)—9

Zesty—Cobis Products Co., Atlanta, GA—42, 52

Zetz—Zetz 7-Up Bottling Co., New Orleans, LA—24, 38

Zill's—(see Minnekahta)—38

Zing—42

Zipps—Cleveland, OH—65, 67

Zweifel's—New Glarus Bottling Works. An etched glass exists.